GRIVAS
PORTRAIT
of a *TERRORIST*

Dudley Barker # GRIVAS
PORTRAIT
of a # TERRORIST

Harcourt, Brace and Company, New York

ILLUSTRATIONS

GRIVAS
PORTRAIT
of a *TERRORIST*

CHAPTER I

DURING THE Greek Orthodox Easter in May 1959 a small, slightly-built, elderly man in a grey suit, accompanied by his stolid, white-haired wife, and by a colonel of the Greek Army seconded as his aide-de-camp, was driven into a large barracks on the outskirts of Athens. In the powerful, battered-looking car that followed were six powerful, battered-looking security policemen; and sprinkled among the crowds of officers, soldiers and their families who had gathered to celebrate Easter were secret service agents. When the small, elderly man got out of his car, the soldiers greeted him as a national hero, shouting his assumed name, 'DI-GHE-NIS!' and that of his terrorist organization, 'E-O-KA!' Generals rushed forward in homage. The soldiers, when given permission, hoisted him on to a table top while they shouted his praises, and a four-piece wind orchestra wailed through a loudspeaker the national patriotic songs of Greece. Later in the day, when he wanted to hurry from one engagement to another, the Greek Air Force (to the annoyance, it was said, of the Greek Prime Minister when he heard of it) placed a helicopter at his disposal. He was treated like the saviour, if not the leader, of his country; hailed as the greatest of the Pan-Hellenes, the hero of a nation, the liberator. The King of Greece, who had just visited the same barracks, had been received far more sedately. Yet George Grivas held no official

position. He was a retired lieutenant-colonel, now promoted to the rank of retired general. This is not an
unusual rank in Greece, where there are more than 1,000
retired generals; partly because an officer retired on
account of war wounds receives the time promotion and,
of course, the increased pension of his class, until he
becomes a retired general. It is said that anyone who
enters any coffee-shop in Central Athens and calls '*Mon
general*' will jerk the head of every other man there.

George Grivas had not acquired his position by those
means, however. What he had done—the reason for the
hysterical hero-worship that greeted him in Greece at
that time—was to lead an underground terrorist organization called E.O.K.A. in Cyprus for four years in an
attempt to force Britain to surrender her island colony
into union with Greece. As a result of his actions, some
600 people were killed—most of them murdered, and
more than half of them Greek. One thousand, two
hundred and sixty people were wounded.

Four thousand, seven hundred and fifty-eight bombs
were prepared. Of these, 927 caused major damage, 855
minor damage—and 2,976 either failed to explode or
were discovered by the security forces before they could
be used. The material damage wrought, and the damage
to the island's economy, amounted to millions of pounds.
The sum that Grivas's backers spent on E.O.K.A. and his
terrorist campaign was not much more than £50,000.

All this murderous and violent activity failed to achieve
its political objective. By the London Agreement that
ended the unhappy business early in 1959, union of
Cyprus with Greece was ruled out. But in the course of
the struggle the N.A.T.O. alliance on which the safety
of Europe depends had been threatened with disruption.

A war between Greece and Turkey had not been wholly impossible. The traditionally warm friendship between the British and the Greeks had been severely strained, and might be a long time mending. And a whole generation of Cypriot children had been corrupted into a delight in indiscipline, violence and murder.

Grivas conducted his activities according to a careful military plan which he had worked out several years earlier and meticulously prepared. But to the Greeks, in Cyprus and in Greece itself, he appeared rather as the spontaneous character whom Greeks love, the patriot-bandit. He caught the imagination of his fellow-countrymen, partly by striving for Pan-Hellenism, the century-old Greek longing to have all the scattered Greek populations under the national flag, but mostly by the skill with which he eluded capture, for four years, by considerable forces of British troops and police. He became a contemporary Robin Hood legend. When he finally came out of hiding in March of 1959, he remarked to a Greek journalist, 'It was not easy to face a mighty empire within the confines of a small island'. The British themselves had praised the feat. Field-Marshal Sir John (afterwards Lord) Harding, who strove for two years to catch Grivas, and twice nearly succeeded in smashing his terrorist organization, described him as 'a man of great personal courage and endurance, a stern disciplinarian and austere in his habits'. The British officers who led the chase of his guerrillas through the Cyprus mountains conceded his considerable military skill.

In a talk to one of his friends, shortly after his return to Athens, Grivas said: 'I was the man exactly qualified for the job. To start with, I am a trained soldier'—he was, indeed, a staff lecturer in tactics—'and therefore, when I

9

was opposed by Regular soldiers, and well supplied with intelligence of their movements, I could work out on the map what they were about to do and either avoid it or frustrate it. Secondly, I had considerable experience of guerrilla fighting against the Communists in Greece. Thirdly, I am a Cypriot.'

In stature, Grivas is quite remarkably tiny, though he has large hands, which he throws about jerkily while talking; all his movements are abrupt and jerky. The top of his head is bald, with a fringe of grey hair at the back and sides. From behind, one notices that his bald scalp is wrinkled, like that of a much older man; when he returned to Greece he was nearing his sixty-first birthday. Facially, he does not much resemble the description put out by the Cyprus Government on the 'Wanted' police poster which, in 1956, offered £10,000 and a free, secret passage to anywhere in the world for information leading to his arrest. The poster described him as 'about fifty-eight years old, small Hitler-type moustache, large ears set low on his head'.

It is not, however, his ears that are noticeable, but his large, dark, darting eyes, under thick, dark brows. They move continually, his glance jerking from one direction to another like a bird's. The moustache is very much larger, thicker, heavier—a dark grey bar across the top lip—than the description implies. The similarity is not with Hitler, but Groucho Marx. Except for the baldness of his head, indeed, Grivas's likeness to Groucho Marx is irrepressible.

The man's small body is as tough as nylon. The story was widely circulated during the terrorist campaign that Grivas was a sick man. He had, it was categorically stated, a weak heart, diabetes, and an ulcer. None of this was true. He has the sort of wiry good health that enables him to run up a hill twice as fast as a man half his age. He eats very little, as a matter of habit; in Cyprus, he reduced that little to still less. He never ate meat, though he could often have had it in the villages. His chief food was fruit. 'It was thanks to this fruit that I kept alive', he said. 'I ate as many as twenty-four oranges a day.' Somebody asked, 'Why exactly twenty-four? Why not twenty-three, or twenty-five?' To this Grivas replied, 'I regulated my eating by my watch. I ate two oranges every hour. And that's how I kept in good health and kept up my resistance.'

Apart from an occasional bout of diarrhoea, the chief ill-health from which he suffered in Cyprus was tooth-ache. Three of his teeth rotted, and for considerable periods he had to put up with the toothache, since he could not get to a dentist for treatment. He related that on one occasion a dentist was brought to a house where he was hiding. While he was filling his tooth, the house was surrounded by British troops—whether by accident or whether because they had been tipped off, Grivas did not know. All seemed lost. But, he said, the god of E.O.K.A. saved him; he did not specify how.

This anecdote greatly intrigued the Greeks, and many versions of it are now current. The most picturesque is that, as the soldiers came in, the dentist with great presence of mind put the chloroform mask over Grivas's face and pretended the patient was unconscious. In fact, there were some E.O.K.A. men posted outside—as there always were when Grivas ventured into an exposed position—and they created a diversion that drew off the troops, while Grivas himself slipped away in another direction. (An interesting tail-piece to the anecdote is that six Cypriot dentists have claimed to be the dentist in question.)

Of the toothache, however, there is no doubt. One of the first men Grivas saw when he got to Greece was his brother-in-law, a doctor, who examined him and pronounced him fit, but about a stone under weight. Among other early visitors was a dentist, who removed five decayed roots from his jaw.

The austerity of his diet he extends to his personal life. He never smokes, and rarely drinks alcohol, even a glass of light wine. He sleeps little, and every morning on rising, no matter where he may be, goes through a long, regular set of physical exercises. He has only one relaxation—he is an enthusiastic, almost fanatical, collector of stamps. During the course of his life he has filled many albums, and one of his first questions on arriving in Athens was as to their safety. He continued his hobby of stamp-collecting throughout the terrorist campaign in the mountains of Cyprus. It was his one pleasure. People in Nicosia frequently bought stamps from the local dealer, and they were sent, by the courier system which was his elaborate method of communication, to wherever he happened to be hiding. And there his fellow terrorists watched him examine the stamps with a magnifying glass. His letters, sent by a secret route to Andreas Azinas, his chief contact in Athens, often contained foreign stamps to be added to his collection and kept for his return. When he finally came out of hiding, in that curious—and curiously new—uniform of E.O.K.A. beret, green cardigan, breeches, short boots, pistol and binoculars, his pockets were stuffed with foreign stamps.

Stamps were also his relaxation in the hectic first weeks of his return to Greece. He soon left his small, rather poverty-stricken flat in the bourgeois Athenian district of Thyssion, and moved out to borrowed villas in two of the distant suburbs; he continued to live a conspiratorial kind of life, moving his residence without warning, followed by a bodyguard who were instructed never to mention the place at which he was, or the time at which he might arrive anywhere. In the outlying suburbs, assisted by some of his old assassin comrades who acted as his secretaries, he started to write his memoirs, for which, he confided to an intimate friend on a journey he made to Rhodes, he expected to receive from American publishers three or four times what the whole E.O.K.A. terrorist campaign cost its sponsors, about 50 per cent. more than Field-Marshal Montgomery got for his memoirs. Grivas says he will devote the whole sum to orphans of E.O.K.A. men who were killed. In between bouts of literary work, he got out his stamp album and relaxed with magnifying glass and tweezers.

When Grivas remarked that, at a time of great danger to himself in Cyprus, the god of E.O.K.A. had saved him, he did not mean this remark frivolously. He regards himself as a highly religious man. He goes very often to church. By some curious distortion of values, he completely persuaded himself that his murderous adventure not only had the blessing of the local Church (as indeed it had), but of the Almighty. The letters which, by undisclosed routes, he sent back from the Cypriot mountains to fellow conspirators in Athens, expressed his unswerving faith, even in his most perilous moments, that God would save him from capture, and would lead his venture to success. 'It was as though', says one of the conspirators, 'he had a contract with God.' And Grivas imbued many of his associates in Cyprus with this same extraordinary belief. One of them, when told that Grivas was surrounded, without ammunition, and with most of his lieutenants either killed or captured, replied quite sincerely, 'But he still has the Holy Virgin with him.' This is not quite so blasphemous as it sounds, in the peculiar context of the Greek Orthodox Church, which for centuries has been largely identified with a mystical, vague Greek patriotism.

Everything Grivas does, he does with a fanaticism that verges on the insane. He is a man with a fixity of purpose which he follows with irrational intensity. On the one hand, he is a fanatical assassin, with not the slightest scruple about any human life that stands in his way. In another context, he is a fanatical stamp-collector and a fanatical devotee of physical exercises which he carries out at inordinate length every morning. He is fanatically anti-Communist—almost pathologically so—to an extent unjustified even by the terrible sufferings which the Greek Communists inflicted on their countrymen during and after the Second World War. Mixed up with this is his religious fanaticism, which is so associated with Greek patriotism as to be almost identified with it. And added to all this is a fanatical lust for personal power— not for wealth, for which he cares nothing, but solely for power. This drive for power has been inflamed by several notable failures during his life to obtain it, and was perhaps the main motive of his actions in Cyprus; that they were carried out with such ruthlessness is partly because the pattern of modern Greek history is violence, from which freedom is expected to spring, and partly because Grivas himself spent many years of his life in conditions in which massacre and violence of every kind were so frequent as to be normal.

The Cyprus Government at one time described him as
'a brutalized and disappointed soldier'—a description
that fits the facts. Before the Second World War he was
regarded in the Greek Army as an exemplary staff officer,
severe in his views on discipline, rigidly correct in military etiquette. His record, during and after the German
occupation of Greece, of violent anti-Communist action,
and indulgence in extreme right-wing politics, ended his
professional career as a soldier. Yet when he tried to
enter politics—he stood at two general elections—he
was a flop. When he went to Cyprus, he was avenging
both those major disappointments of his ambitions. That
he carried out his Cyprus activities with such ruthlessness
was partly due to his usual fanaticism, and partly to the
contempt in which he held human life, including his own.
When, during the war against the Italians in Albania in
1941, his commanding general expressed grief at the
death of another officer whom he had sent forward to
reconnoitre a particularly dangerous area, Grivas said,
'We came here with no guarantee of remaining alive. We
came here to die. We are condemned men here. If we live,
that's fortunate. But the rule is to die, and to live is the
exception.'

It was partly by this grim sort of fatalism and quite
unscrupulous attitude to taking life that Grivas contrived
to keep his terrorist campaign in being in Cyprus, off and
on, for four years. It depended on him and his determination. Although the sponsors of E.O.K.A. say they had
another leader ready to take over should Grivas have been
killed or captured, the fact is that the terrorism would
have ended with him. If he had been caught, the other
terrorists, most of whom were of poor quality, would
have drifted swiftly back into inactivity. For E.O.K.A.

to have a hope of winning, Grivas himself had to remain at large, in spite of the attempts of some 25,000 British troops and a considerable police force to catch him.

How did he do it?

The Greek pilot of the aeroplane in which, in March 1959, he was taken away from Cyprus, asked him that very question. Grivas replied, 'I managed it thanks to God, who protected me, and to the stupidity of the British organization.' There seems to be some justification in the latter half of that reply. Certainly in the earlier part of the Cyprus campaign there were times when Grivas was going about the island quite openly; once, when his car stuck in a muddy roadside ditch, it was obligingly hauled out by a lorry full of British troops who happened to be passing.

Throughout the four years, Grivas did not depend on disguises. He was often called a master of disguise, with the implication that he slipped about Cyprus got up as an old woman, or a priest, or a crippled peasant, or even as a British officer, attending Service dances and leaving bombs under his table. There is an often-repeated story that he disguised himself as a village idiot when Sir John Harding was passing through a certain village, and that he contrived to shake him by the hand—and wrote to him next day to tell him so. But these were just legends, deliberately fostered as part of the build-up of the patriot-bandit figure, upon which the appeal of Grivas to the Greek Cypriots so much depended.

He remained uncaptured, not by disguises, or by any sort of conjuring tricks, but by a meticulously careful plan of hiding. He had long before worked out a military plan of concealment, in great detail, with the precision of a staff officer. Once the British had woken up to the danger of his presence, and started a serious hunt for him, he put this plan into operation, and stuck to it. At one time Sir John Harding nearly took him by surprise, jumping a sudden, large-scale operation at him in the mountains that failed to capture him only by very bad luck. This was because Grivas himself had been, up to that time—early in 1956—a little too complacent. Once he had had that warning, he went to ground in a series of previously constructed hiding-places. He stayed in one of them as long as he could, not stirring, and only moving from it when he was forced to. The risk of his betrayal to the British was very slight, because no more than one or two people at any one time knew where he was; and when he left one hiding-place, he never revealed to the man who had known that one where the next one was. Throughout the terrorist campaign—after the first few months, at least—Grivas was as invisible to most of his own followers as he was to the British. Plenty of E.O.K.A. terrorists who survived the four years never once saw their leader. In the tangled Troodos Mountains, or in the twisting warrens of narrow back streets that comprise the Cyprus towns, a planned campaign of concealment was not so difficult as it appears, particularly after Grivas had swung almost the entire Greek Cypriot population to his side, at first through fear, and afterwards by conviction. A police force is sorely handicapped if it works without the support of the civil population. In Cyprus, it was Grivas who could always count on getting information from the people—and, indeed, from the police themselves, for E.O.K.A. penetrated the police force at a very early stage, and there were occasions when Grivas was hidden in the houses of quite senior Greek Cypriot police officers. It is strongly denied, however—perhaps rather too emphatically denied—that he was ever hidden in the Greek Consulate.

To receive information, and to convey his instructions to his followers, Grivas had an elaborate system of couriers and messengers, most of whom did not know each other, let alone know where Grivas himself was— in which hole in the ground he was concealed, or in which secret priest-hole hollowed out beneath the floor of a house. Towards the end of the four years, the British Intelligence system vastly improved, particularly under General Darling. Grivas's personal security was then nearly broken on at least two occasions by Intelligence methods. On one of them, he was within a couple of yards of being caught, and he escaped only by a combination of his undoubted coolness and daring, and his usual luck.

But for most of the four years his plan of hiding worked with astonishing efficiency, and thus enabled him to carry out his programme of violence and murder, and the most cynical corruption of a whole generation of young people.

CHAPTER II

GEORGE GRIVAS was born in the hospital at Nicosia, the capital town of Cyprus, on 23 May 1898. He was one of the five children—two boys and three girls—of Theodore Grivas, a grocer in the dusty village of Trikomo, about twelve miles north of Famagusta, and just inland from the eastern coast of the island. Since there were few facilities at Trikomo, his mother went to the Nicosia Hospital for the birth of her child, and it was in that town that his name was registered. Three weeks later she took him back to Trikomo, where he spent his early years. Both his parents are now dead, but his brother Michael, a doctor in Nicosia, and two of his sisters are still living.

The incident that George Grivas himself most clearly remembers from his early years at Trikomo was the first time the police arrested him, and the prompt and cunning manner in which he got out of it. A Bishop had been elected who was unpopular; the priesthood in Cyprus was always as much a political issue as a spiritual matter. There was a demonstration in Trikomo, the people booing the Bishop, and in this the infant Grivas eagerly joined by beating a tin can with a stick in order to add to the noise. A policeman ran over and grasped the child. Looking quickly around, young Grivas pointed to the balcony of his father's house. His mother, he lied, had been washing some corn, had spread it on the balcony to dry, and had told him to beat the tin with a stick in order to scare away the birds. No doubt the policeman was not particularly impressed by this tale, but he had too much to do to bother to check it, so he released the boy, who rejoiced a great deal at his cleverness.

When he was old enough, George Grivas was sent to school at the Pancyprian Gymnasium in Cyprus. This school, attended by some 2,000 boys and girls, is the most famous on the island. It was built on Church property, and stands immediately across the road from the Archbishopric of the Greek Orthodox Church in Cyprus; and it is the Church's most important instrument for inculcating into the young people of the leading Cypriot families a spirit of militant Greek patriotism. The British have never prevented such teaching in the schools. There was nothing to prevent a schoolboy at the Pancyprian Gymnasium from writing an essay on the subject, 'The British never leave a country unless there is bloodshed', or his teacher from writing in the margin, 'Bravo! This is the way to liberation'; this is an actual incident. In Grivas's youth the teaching was not so violently anti-British, but was nevertheless grounded on the theme that Cyprus belonged to Greece, and that all Greek patriots should strive for Enosis—union—with the mother-country. This teaching does not, however, seem to have had much influence on George Grivas as a pupil. He was quite undistinguished until almost the end of his school life, when he was in the Sixth Form; even then, the incident that brought him recognition was not academic. At the school sports that year the 100 metres race was confidently expected to be won by a tall boy with very long legs named Hadjidimitriou, who was later to become a physical training instructor and a Greek poet of note under the name of Glafcos Alithersis. But to everybody's astonishment, the race was won by a diminutive boy with very short legs, George Grivas. This gained him a schoolboy reputation, and it is about all that his fellow pupils can now recall of him at school.

Although his youth was passed in the peacefulness of the island of Cyprus, the world around it was turbulent; particularly the Greek world. When he was fourteen, the Balkan Wars broke out, in which the Greek Army gained renown. The Greek state doubled its territory and its population in Europe—though more than 2 million Greeks still lived under alien, mostly Turkish rule and many were suffering oppression. All young men of Greek blood were inspired by the military glory of the victories, and filled with ardour to free those who were still subjugated. In the quiet island of Cyprus, of course, the Greeks under British rule were not oppressed at all. There is no evidence that the young Grivas felt any impulse to link himself with Greek nationalism in Cyprus. What he then decided was to become a true Greek by naturalization, and a professional soldier in the Greek Army.

As he grew through his 'teens, there was plenty to reinforce such resolves. The First World War threw Greece into chaos, the pro-German King Constantine trying to keep neutral, and the statesman Venizelos splitting the country, but at last bringing the Greek Army into battle with brilliant success on the Allied side. No doubt the young Grivas was torn between his loyalty to Constantine and his dislike of Venizelos—he was always a royalist, and always anti-liberal. But this did not turn him aside from his purpose. He left Cyprus in 1916 still an island of peacefulness, and went to Athens, where he became a cadet at the Military Academy. He took this step, it is said, against the wishes of his father.

George Grivas finished his course at the cadet school and was gazetted as a lieutenant in the Greek Army on 26 August 1919. A month later he was posted to the 30th Infantry Regiment. It was a time of great satisfaction for a Greek. Venizelos, who had become a world statesman at the Peace Conference in Paris, had gained permission for Greece to occupy Smyrna, in Asia Minor, and, heartily supported by Mr. Lloyd George, was soon to be given a mandate over Thrace and the north-western area of Asia Minor as well. By August 1920, in a treaty that was never to be ratified, Greece was given the whole of Thrace, the Aegean islands she already held, and the Smyrna district. The only two shadows were that the Greek troops who formed part of the expedition to south Russia to fight the Bolsheviks were suffering heavy losses, and in Turkey the Nationalists under Mustapha Kemal were preparing to oppose the Greek entry into Asia Minor. Mustapha Kemal, indeed, soon set up an alternative government at Ankara and challenged the treaty that gave the territory to Greece. The Greek General Staff were confident, however, that they could establish Greek rule in all the assigned territory within three months, and at the end of March 1921 set out to do so.

The campaign was a disaster. At first all seemed to go well, but at that time the only opposition came from bands of Turkish guerrillas. By June, the Greeks were within sixty miles of Ankara. The more prudent Greek generals thought it advisable to pause there, but the politicians urged that Ankara must be taken, so the Army pressed on, very weak though it was in transport and communications, over a waterless desert, until it reached the Sakharia River, behind which Mustapha Kemal had his army dug in. In August the Greek soldiers, who had suffered tremendous privations and hardships, and were short of almost everything from food to ammunition, attacked the Turkish positions and were badly defeated, with very heavy casualties. In spite of all this, the Greeks held for another year the line at a distance of sixty miles from Ankara, while their politicians rushed to Europe to try to get a negotiated peace. In August 1922 the Turks attacked, routed the Greek Army, sacked and burned Smyrna, and massacred most of its Greek inhabitants.

These horrors were Grivas's introduction to warfare. He saw six months' service as a lieutenant of infantry in Asia Minor, and was decorated for bravery. His personal part had been unexceptionable, but he had seen a Greek army overthrown very largely because of interference from politicians, mismanagement of supplies, dissension of a political kind among the senior officers, with its consequent lack of discipline, and inadequate planning. These were lessons he was not to forget. And soon he received another—that in the chaos that follows a war, and particularly a defeat, the established order can easily be overthrown by force. For the Liberal officers of the defeated army angrily and successfully demanded the abdication (for the second time) of King Constantine in favour of the Crown Prince, who thus became George II. And a Revolutionary Committee brought the Commander-in-Chief, three former Prime Ministers and two former Ministers before a court martial, which sentenced them to death. They were pushed into lorries and taken outside Athens, where they were immediately shot. Britain was so horror-struck that she broke off diplomatic relations with Greece.

It was in this atmosphere of defeat, disaster, violence and revenge that Grivas began his career as a regular officer. It seems to have aroused from him no political comment, but to have persuaded him to devote himself with grim intensity to the job of soldiering. He began to specialize in the study of infantry tactics, and was twice sent on special courses to France. One of the Greek officers who accompanied him recalls him as very reserved, very serious, and concentrating on his studies. He never went to cabarets or had anything to do with women, rarely drank even a glass of wine, and never smoked. He was intimate with nobody, and seems to have been completely humourless. On his return to Greece he was posted to various regiments, and finally became a lecturer on tactics at the High School of War at Athens. He was there when the Second World War began—a staff officer of somewhat academic qualifications and a reserved, unsocial nature. At the end of 1939 he was placed on the General Staff of the Army.

There had, however, been one softer passage in his life. While he was on regimental duties he was in 1929 at Missolonghi. One day the niece of one of his brother officers, Eustace Dekas, came to pay her uncle a visit. Her name was Kiki (short for Vassiliki),the daughter of a pharmacist called Dekas, and she came from the nearby mountain village of Proussos. She was introduced to Grivas, and, as he himself puts it, they felt a mutual attraction. Kiki was a good-looking girl, younger than he, and a creditable performer on the piano. There was, however, no hasty match. Shortly afterwards the young officer left on his two courses of study in France. It was not until eleven years later that the wedding took place. Grivas was then a staff lecturer at the High School of

War in Athens. Kiki's father had a chemist's shop in the bourgeois Athenian district of Thyssion, as he still has. For this reason, the Grivases set up house in the same district. They took the second floor flat of a brown stucco building at No. 4 Nileos Street, just off the small Thyssion Square. In the flat below lives a very elderly retired general who was Grivas's teacher when he was a cadet. Next door is a shoe shop. Dekas the chemist is just over the way. Nearby are a grocer's and a café, all rather dusty and shabby, though not as poor as further down the hill. Thyssion, which is one of the oldest parts of Athens, lies beneath the Acropolis, in an area of quite extensive public gardens and open spaces on the hillside, traditional places for young Athenians to make love. It is here, among a population of civil servants, Army officers, shopkeepers and such, that the Grivases have lived ever since.

The marriage, though childless, has been a happy one. Mrs. Grivas, now white-haired, rather stocky in build, perhaps somewhat stolid in temperament, regards her husband with admiration and devotion, and accepts without question whatever opinion he may form. During the four years he was in Cyprus she lived in anxious seclusion, seeing very few people except her family. She sacked her maid, partly because she wanted to be solitary, and partly to economize. She had not even the consolation of her piano, since the Communists had destroyed it during the fighting in 1944, and she had never been able to afford a new one.

In the nearly two decades during which George Grivas had been pursuing an unexciting career in the Army, rising from a young lieutenant with decorations for gallantry to a middle-aged colonel on the staff, Greece had been following its usual turbulent course. In the nineteen-twenties the country had somehow managed to absorb the flood of Greek refugees from Turkey, under an agreement to exchange minorities; had rejected King George II, who went into exile; and set up a republic, succeeded by a dictatorship, which in turn gave place to another republic. In the nineteen-thirties Greece was governed for a time by Venizelos, threw off an attempted revolution, and restored King George II to the throne, under whom and with whose consent, General Metaxas in 1936 established himself as dictator. It was the dictator Metaxas who, on 28 October 1940, answered with a resounding 'No' an ultimatum from Mussolini and sent the Greek Army north to meet the Italian invasion from Albania.

For two weeks the Italians advanced, aiming at Jannina on the road to Athens, and Florina in the direction of Salonika. But they then met the first Greek divisions forming the line in the mountains. By 14 November the Italians had been held everywhere. Within a few days the Greeks, reinforced by fresh divisions moving north, were on the attack and were throwing the invaders back into Albania. The Greeks captured the chief Italian base at Koritaza on 22 November. Argyrocastro fell on 8 December. By the end of the month, in conditions of exceptional wintry severity in the Albanian mountains, the Greeks halted for a while, and prepared to receive the Italian counter-attack.

This was the time, of course, when the only people fighting the Axis were the British and the Greeks. This was the unexpected resistance, carried out with great fortitude and gallantry, which is said to have thrown Hitler's time-table out so badly that he had to postpone his attack on Russia by six weeks.

In this campaign Colonel Grivas played an honourable, if not particularly distinguished, role. At the beginning he was in the operations office of the General Staff. But during December he was appointed Chief of Staff of the 2nd (Athens) Division, commanded by a somewhat elderly officer, Major-General George Lavdas. This 2nd Division, sometimes called by Greeks the Iron Division, was part of the 1st Army Corps, and was in action among the mountains on the left centre of the Epirus front. By the time Colonel Grivas joined it, it had already fought its way across the Albanian border, and was moving towards a position on the right bank of the River Drina, a few miles north of Argyrocastro, which was as far as it got. The Division, which had no motor transport at all, and depended entirely on mules, took its fair share of hardship, and provided its fair share of fighting, without being in any particularly notable battle.

Officers who served under Grivas vividly recall the arrival of their new Chief of Staff. He was tireless in his activity, and demanded as much from everybody. He made ceaseless tours of the front, either on foot or, when possible, by mule. He soon became virtually the commander of the Division, for General Lavdas seems to have been happy to hand over a good deal to this younger, more vigorous officer. He gained the respect of his staff, but not their affection, for he was severe in the execution of duty, and austere in himself. He never played cards, never joined in the singing of a song, never drank alcohol, or even smoked a cigarette. 'None of us became his friend', says one of the officers, who now holds high Army rank, 'because nobody could be his friend. One could not discuss anything with him except matters of duty. We respected him, but he was too austere for any

27

intimacy. In every other man I know, I could point to some weakness or other. But Grivas seemed to have none, either of character or in his profession as a soldier. As for relaxations—he never relaxed.'

In the early months of 1941 the Italians launched their big counter-attack under the personal supervision of Mussolini. The Greeks held it everywhere. Neither the appalling weather in the mountains nor the superior equipment of the Italians could daunt them. They were, indeed, preparing for a further advance, with the intention of throwing the Italians out of Albania, when, on 6 April, Germany also declared war on Greece. The issue was then decided. In spite of the meagre reinforcements the British could put into the country, the German advance was almost unchecked. The Greek Army in Albania began to pull back, and it was in the retreat that the 2nd Division had its hardest battles, fending off the Italians; it was never engaged with the Germans. It is the testimony of Divisional officers that Colonel Grivas, although he had an injured arm, was with the rearguard of the Division throughout the retreat. It is hinted that the discipline he imposed was of the severest, and that he did not stop at summary execution, with his revolver, of any soldier who deserted his post before the order came.

The Germans cut off the Greek Army retiring from Albania. It consisted of three army corps. The commander of the 3rd Corps, a Lieut.-General Tsolacoglou, having come to an understanding with the commanders of the 1st and 2nd, and, having consulted the local Bishop of Jannina, then mutinied. He removed the Army Commander, General Pitsicas, from his post, and set about negotiating capitulation to the Germans. The Greek Commander-in-Chief, General Papagos, signalled that the

Army Commander was to be reinstated at once, and the Army was to continue fighting. So did the King himself. Tsolacoglou disobeyed these orders and surrendered to the Germans. General Pitsicas returned to Athens, where he still wanders about, a smiling old man of nearly eighty, one of the many retired generals, treated with great respect.

The 2nd Division, like all the others, had, of course, to lay down its arms, and was given a time and place in which to do so. One of the regiments, commanded by an officer named Katsotas (who is now mayor of Athens), gave up its arms, in contradiction to the agreement, on the orders of a German patrol led by a corporal. When Colonel Grivas heard of this he beat his head with his fists and wept. His whole conception of military discipline was outraged. He threatened that he would have taken action against Katsotas had it not been for one fact: Katsotas held one rank higher than Grivas, who was therefore restrained by his respect for military obedience.

The Greek soldiers who had fought such a gallant war were disarmed and sent marching back to their bases. The Bishop of Jannina later rose high in the Greek Church, and became a leading figure in the campaign to unite Cyprus with Greece, making several violently anti-British speeches to the Athenian mob. Tsolacoglou, as reward for his mutiny, became Germany's puppet Prime Minister of Greece. And after a time the officers of the 2nd Division found themselves back in occupied Athens, which was soon to be starving.

CHAPTER III

UNTIL THIS time, none of the actors in the drama had behaved dishonourably; and even in the moment of surrender, and in the disintegration of values that followed, it is difficult to apportion blame. For the tragedy of Greece was not submerged in the general tragedy of occupied Europe, but was of a special kind. The Greeks had fought, unexpectedly and against hopeless odds, with skill and great gallantry, the 2nd Division as valiantly as the rest, and, of its officers, Colonel Grivas with more determination and grim sense of duty than most. The nation had been militarily overthrown, not betrayed; there was no fifth column in Greece. The King had escaped with his Government, performing a last act of bravery in the evacuation from Crete; Metaxas, the dictator, had died early in the year, when the Greek victories over the Italians were most flourishing. The occupiers, in so far as they were Italian, were held by all Greeks in contempt, and in so far as they were German, were regarded with either a stunned apathy or defiance. It was a tragedy of the same special kind as that which might have taken place had the British Isles been conquered. Indeed, the traditionally warm friendship between Britain and Greece became almost fanatical then and after the war; which underlines the unhappiness of the more recent divergence, of which Grivas was the cause and instigator.

When Greece was jointly occupied by the Germans and the Italians—with the latter given a rather larger share of administration—there were very many Greeks determined to carry on resistance. But there was only one group with any organization to do so. This was the Communist Party, which had managed to keep an underground network in being during the years of Metaxas's dictatorship. Once Germany attacked Russia, the Communist Party was very ready for armed resistance. It organized a political movement of the left, known by its Greek initials as E.A.M., and this in turn recruited guerrilla bands in the mountains over most of Greece, and particularly in those areas which were of most importance to the German lines of communication. These bands were welded into a guerrilla army, known by its initials as E.L.A.S. And very soon E.A.M. and E.L.A.S., although they included many radicals who were by no means Communist and many peasants who simply fought because they were told to, came securely under the control of the Communist Party of Greece. When British officers were later parachuted into the country to bring arms and money and leadership to the partisans, it was with E.L.A.S. that, for obvious military reasons, they had chiefly to co-operate. There were, as time went on, only two other sizeable guerrilla organizations actually in the field with whom the British could, and did, co-operate. These were E.D.E.S., the democratic, republican force which General Zervas kept in being in the north-west of Greece until the end of the war, and E.K.K.A., the armed force of the moderate centre, which Colonel Psaros put into the field in central Greece in 1943, and which was wiped out by E.L.A.S., and Psaros himself murdered, in the following spring. Apart from

Zervas, therefore, the only effective resistance in the mountains of Greece throughout most of the occupation was E.L.A.S., under Communist orders.

In Athens itself, in the early days of bitterness and confusion, numerous small and ineffective groups of people were formed with the rather vague idea of resistance to the Germans, without much comprehension of how to do it, or what it involved. One of these groups was started by General Lavdas, former commander of the 2nd Division, and his Chief of Staff, Colonel Grivas. It had no name, few members, and very sketchy objects and resources. But, like most such scratch teams, its original purposes were worthy. General Lavdas soon dropped out. The reason is not now clear, but Grivas maintains they separated because Lavdas wanted to hesitate, to postpone action, and Grivas wanted to get fighting as soon as possible. It is also held that Grivas's appointment was advised by an unnamed British agent. There is no record of this on the British side, but in Athens at that time there were many people who either were, or said they were, agents of the British, and one of these may have reasonably recommended that command of the group should be turned over to the man who wanted to get into action, and who was also a professional soldier with a good record.

The Communists, at about this time, also thought Grivas was worth having. They were doing their best to recruit regular officers for their forces in the mountains, though it was not until 1943 that they got their commander-in-chief, the able General Saraphis, by compulsion, and a number of other professional officers who had no Communist sympathies, but were persuaded by various means to join the most powerful force actually fighting the Germans. It was earlier than this that an approach was made to Grivas, through a journalist working on a right-wing underground newspaper. Grivas arrived at the home of the journalist, dressed in a blue raincoat, and with military boots under his civilian trousers—he even then had an aptitude for semi-uniform of picturesque kind—and was cautiously led through the streets to the house of a Communist journalist, Constantine Vidalis. When they were all safely in, two Communist leaders appeared. The two journalists retired for two hours to the kitchen, while discussions continued. When it was dark, and they could walk through the streets together, Grivas left with the first journalist, and told him, on the way, 'They have asked me to command for them. I am to consider it. But you can tell them that I think the answer will be "No".'

How much Grivas and the few officers loosely grouped around him actually did to resist the Germans in the early stages of the occupation is uncheckable. Grivas himself maintains that his organization—though at the time it scarcely warranted that term—was quite active. His chief assistant, a rather fat, smiling Greek officer named Homer Papadopoulos, then a captain, but now a lieutenant-colonel, claims that the group carried out extensive sabotage in warehouses and among military stores, and damaged some shipping in Piraeus Harbour. He says, also, that a complete guerrilla unit of ex-officers was sent into the nearby mountains of Kitheron to await an expected parachute drop of weapons from the British, and that, although they waited for ten days, the arms did not arrive. It seems that Grivas had suggested to the exiled Greek Government that it would be a good idea to have an efficient armed band so near to Athens, to protect the capital, in any emergency, from Communist capture; even then he was thinking in terms of opposition to the Communists rather than to the Germans. But the Greek Government was persuaded that it might be equally dangerous to have Athens in the hands of Colonel Grivas himself, and did not go ahead with the plan. This embittered Grivas against Greek politicians.

A few officers were then sent singly into the mountains, Papadopoulos says, to link up with existing groups. They were either killed or driven away by the Communists, and this embittered Grivas towards the Communist Party.

Later in the occupation, Grivas worked out a plan for holding a beach-head in the Peloponnese to enable British troops to land back in Greece. He based his plan on a series of underground hides that would be secretly prepared in advance, and guaranteed that, with 1,000 Greeks, mostly ex-officers, he would hold the beach-head for one week. One of the associates of Grivas at this time was an Athenian lawyer named Zafiris Valvis. He made his way to the Middle East, and took the beach-head plan with him. Whether it ever reached the British seems uncertain. In any case, nothing came of it. The disappointment helped to embitter Grivas against the British.

Grivas and his organization soon existed only in Athens, and engaged in less and less resistance to the occupiers. There is some evidence, chiefly from a Greek who was a radio operator for British intelligence in Greece during the war, that shortly before the liberation Grivas accepted arms from the Germans with which to fight the Communists. The Germans would have been, of course, only too pleased, at such small cost, to add to

the chaos into which the country would fall once it was
liberated by the British. Grivas and his followers had by
then no doubt of their true enemy—the Communists.
They became the core of anti-Communist activities in
Greece, the nucleus of the extreme right wing.

Grivas's fears for the future were certainly well
founded. The Communist plan, on the liberation, was to
take over control of the whole of Greece, which would
then become another Soviet satellite. In the resistance
army, E.L.A.S., they seemed to have the strength to do so.
It numbered some 40,000 men, and when it finally disarmed, it agreed to yield up 41,500 rifles, 2,015 machine
guns, 163 mortars and 32 pieces of artillery, and was
known to have large caches of arms still at its disposal in
various parts of Greece. Even during the war the Communists had shown their hand. In the autumn of 1943,
when they mistakenly thought the Germans were about
to pull out of the country, they made a bid to seize
power which was thwarted by the German Army. It was
quite sure, when liberation came, they would make another
attempt, and it was difficult to see much to stop them.

To Grivas, and to many others in Athens, this seemed
a far more appalling prospect than the German occupation. One day the Germans would be driven out. But if
Greece fell under Soviet domination, who could say
when, if ever, freedom would be re-established there?
This thought was torture to Grivas, fanatically religious
and fanatically royalist. He therefore began to group his
followers into a more coherent organization, and at some
time it acquired a name. At a meeting of some of its
members it was said that it must be the unknown organization. Therefore they adopted as its title the mathe-
matical symbol for the unknown, X, which in Greek is

pronounced 'khee'. It was as the leader of the X organization, at about the time of the liberation of the country
by the British, that Colonel Grivas first became known
outside Greece. And he did not acquire a savoury reputation. The most authoritative account of what happened
in Greece was written by Colonel C. M. Woodhouse, who
for much of the time commanded the Allied Military
Mission to the Greek guerrillas. This is what he said, in
his book, *Apple of Discord*, about Grivas and X:

'There were those who saw the political implications of
the occupation too late to exploit them as they would
have wished if they had seen them earlier. . . . An example
is an organization of which much has been heard since
the occupation under the name "X". This body, later
known as the direct-action instrument of the Royalist
right wing under the leadership of Colonel Grivas, has
claimed to have been a resistance movement during the
occupation. If that claim were true, it would be classifi-
able as the only resistance organization of the right then
active in Athens; but in fact its name was unknown until
shortly before the Germans left; and even then the name
signified nothing connected with resistance. Only in the
years immediately after the war did it acquire significance:
the sinister significance of a Ku Klux Klan.'

It is claimed that X had, in fact, one link with the
British which Colonel Woodhouse does not mention.
There was a meeting, it is said, in the autumn of 1943, at
10 Anagnostopoulou Street in Athens, attended by ten
nationalist groups—not Communist—who were to link
up. The meeting, it is claimed, was attended by a Captain
Donald Stott, a New Zealand officer, who got the ten
groups to sign an agreement; Grivas signed for X.

Captain Stott was in Athens at that time, as Colonel

Woodhouse mentions in his book. He had been sent there to carry out sabotage. 'His courage and originality soon involved him in other, far more perilous, activities, in the process of which his political associations were largely of the extreme right. One of them was General Pagagos, Chief of the General Staff under Metaxas in 1940-1; another, far less inoffensive, was the Mayor of Athens installed by the Germans. Through the latter he found himself entering into negotiations of a complicated character with the German occupation authorities. These communications were abruptly severed when they came to the notice of higher British authorities, who had not at first understood their gravity. But sufficient had already happened to convict British policy, in the eyes of malevolent critics, of collusion with the enemy.'

This, then, is Grivas's claim for X to have been known to the British as a resistance movement long before the liberation. While it is a little unfair to expect him to have known that the activities of the British officer with whom he says he had dealings would be 'abruptly severed' when the higher authorities realized what was going on, it does provide some further circumstantial evidence that Grivas and X were already moving in circles that knew collaboration with the Germans. Grivas's antipathy to the Communists, and fear of what they would do to Greece, had become an obsession. He did not, and could not hope to, command any force sufficient to do battle with E.L.A.S. But he could organize X as a terrorist group. And this he proceeded to do.

CHAPTER IV

IN NUMBERS, the strength of the X organization was
trifling. Grivas had at his disposal some 300 men, of
whom about half were ex-officers, and many were cadets.
He divided Athens into fifteen districts, in each of which
was an X group about twenty strong, and a group
leader. Grivas himself ran the organization from headquarters in his flat at Thyssion, though he rarely slept
there when trouble started, but moved about into various
houses in the district where lived friends who would
hide him. His chief lieutenant, Homer Papadopoulos,
was also commander of the 10th X group, in the fashion-
able Kolanaki district of Athens. X was armed mostly
with revolvers, but had a few machine guns and grenades.
These they frequently carried on street-barrows, which
were a common form of transport during the occupation.
The weapons were hidden under what the barrow was
carrying. Whatever the strength of collaboration between
X and the Germans, it did not extend to permission to
carry arms in the street. Papadopolous relates two stories
about this. On one occasion he and two others—one of
them a girl—were carrying weapons from one Athenian
house to another, hidden under some crockery in a
wooden box. The taxi was stopped by a German patrol,
who demanded to know what was in the box. In handing
it out, the X men deliberately let it fall, so that the china
broke. The girl started to weep and bemoan the breakage

of her crockery. The Germans, with an embarrassed shrug, passed by.

The second story illustrates the nervous speed with which Grivas dives for cover if he thinks he is threatened. The organization had four rifles hidden in a dairy, in a building which was suddenly to be taken over by the S.S. The problem was how to get the rifles out. At that time the puppet Greek Government had recruited some security battalions of Greek soldiers, and Greek Army uniforms were not, therefore, immediately suspect. Four X men went into the dairy, put on their own old uniforms, handcuffed Papadopoulos, shouldered the rifles, and marched him away as though he had just been arrested. At a safe distance they vanished into a house to emerge as civilians when the rifles had been stowed away. But several Athenians had seen Papadopoulos apparently under arrest. They at once informed Grivas, who, sure that he must be compromised if his closest associate was arrested, at once dispersed the whole organization and himself took to cover. It also illuminates his character to know that, when he was at last found and told what had happened, he could see no funny side to the incident at all, but flew into a violent rage.

Amusing and light-hearted stories were not, however, typical of the X organization's activities. From the somewhat slender security of houses in the better-off districts of Athens, Grivas was launching his followers into a sporadic war of assassination against the Communists. In the circumstances of the time he commanded a good deal of support from ordinary Athenians. Over most of Greece, the Communist-controlled E.L.A.S. had slaughtered its Greek opponents ruthlessly in a bid for control of the nation. Assassination in revenge did not seem much of a crime. The hard core of X fighters, therefore, was from the first surrounded by an indefinite but quite sizeable number of more or less active supporters. A year or so later these were estimated to number perhaps 200,000, though most of these would have taken very little part in any actions.

The reason for the support that Grivas drew from a large part of the Athenian population was the second attempt by the Communists to use E.L.A.S. to take over the country. As the Germans began withdrawing from Greece in September 1944, and it became evident that the day of liberation was close, E.L.A.S., which by then controlled almost all of Greece except the north-western corner occupied by Zervas, and the capital city, began to close in around Athens. The sporadic, house-to-house skirmishing between right and left in the outlying districts started to flare into something more like warfare, especially around Thyssion, where Grivas had his headquarters, and where the open spaces were particularly adapted to irregular fighting. By early in October the first British troops had landed in the Peloponnese, and the Germans were pulling out from Athens, which they left on the 12th, also deliberately leaving behind stocks of small arms to add vigour to the civil war which they hoped would break out. The previous day, Grivas had come closest to being assassinated. He and Papadopoulos were being driven in a car on the road that passes below the Acropolis, when they ran into an ambush of about twenty armed men in helmets, who sprang out from behind a wall and opened fire on the car. The driver accelerated promptly. Grivas pulled out his revolver in best melodramatic fashion and claims to have accounted for three of the opponents (which would be good shooting with a revolver; but in most combats enemy casualties tend to be exaggerated). A bullet glanced off an Italian grenade which Papadopoulos was carrying at his hip, and wounded him in the buttock; the grenade itself did not explode. A bullet pierced the tank of the car, which began to spout petrol, but the road from there runs downhill, and they reached Thyssion Square in safety.

On 16 October the first British troops reached Athens. Within a couple of days the Greek Government had returned from exile to its own city, accompanied by Mr. Harold Macmillan, then Minister Resident in the Middle East, and Reginald Leeper, the British Ambassador. Not long after, Mr. Anthony Eden looked in. The small force of British troops under General Scobie was received with delight. E.L.A.S. troops were all round the city, but they seemed friendly enough. This amity, however, was not to last. By the beginning of November Greece was cleared of Germans. By the end of that month, the Greek Communists were obviously preparing their bid for power. Why they hesitated so long has never been satisfactorily explained, for had they struck at Athens before the British arrived, Grivas and his X organization would have been helpless to check them. It has been suggested that the Greek Communists were at this time· acting on their own initiative, without the approval of Moscow, and that it was for this reason that they managed their revolt so clumsily.

The story of the Communist rebellion in Athens in December 1944 and January 1945 has been told so often, and in such detail, that only the barest outline is needed here. By an agreement made previously between all parties at Caserta, the Allied Mediterranean headquarters, E.L.A.S. was placed under the command of the Greek Government directly it returned to Cairo, and the Government then placed it under General Scobie. The security problem was, of course, to disarm the guerrilla army and substitute a national guard which would ensure legal authority throughout the land; the other great problem was to bring in and distribute sufficient supplies to prevent the Greeks starving. By early December it was clear that the Communists would not honour their obligation to place their forces under General Scobie's command, but intended to make a revolution. They stage-managed a huge demonstration in Constitution Square, in the centre of Athens, on Sunday, 3 December. The police lost their heads and fired into the crowd, killing several people. The armed rebellion was then on.

The Communists seemed to have every card. E.L.A.S. controlled nearly all Greece, and was encamped in force on the outskirts of Athens. The small force of British, reinforced by two Greek brigades that had been brought home from exile, was steadily forced back into a very small area in the centre of the city, and this it held only tenuously. Field-Marshal Alexander, flying in to look at the military situation, promised to rush reinforcements from Italy, but had evidently some doubt as to whether they would arrive in time.

It was during this period that Grivas's X fighters, who were attracting now more and more ex-officers to their ranks, joined enthusiastically in the fight alongside the British. This was the battle for which Grivas had been preparing. It could not have been won against E.L.A.S., of course, except by the British troops, without whom Greece would have become a Soviet satellite, and would now be behind the Iron Curtain. The British could drive off the E.L.A.S. troops from any particular district, but were then too few to hold it. Communists filtered back in civilian clothes to resume the fight with weapons they had hidden in the houses. In such circumstances, assistance from Greeks who would fight the Communists was useful, no matter what their politics happened to be.

The X organization had always had its headquarters in the district of Thyssion, where Grivas and his wife occupied their second-storey flat, opposite the chemist's shop kept by old Dekas, Mrs. Grivas's father, and by her sister, who is married to a doctor. The cellar of the chemist's shop was one of the X arsenals, and the arms stored there, under charge of a young Athenian of burning right-wing ardour named Vassili Kouroupos, who now runs a shirt shop in the commercial quarter of the town, ranged upwards from revolvers to mortars. The prize piece, indeed, was an Italian mortar which Kouroupos had acquired by holding a whip-round among his comrades, and raising enough to pay the price which the mortar's Communist owner required.

It was to Thyssion that Grivas now rallied most of his troops. They numbered by then about 300 fighters, and their families made up a total of some 500 to 600 people. The Communists had made one earlier sortie against Thyssion and had penetrated it for a time, but had been driven back with the loss of seven dead.

Now, on 3 December 1944—the day of the demonstration in Constitution Square upon which the police fired, and which started the Communist rebellion in Greece—the Communists came against Thyssion in force. Grivas and his X organization were the only right-wing opponents who could hope to strive with any competence at all in a set battle against the Communist assault. The E.L.A.S. troops attacked from the heights surrounding Thyssion on three sides, and gradually closed in. The battle continued throughout 3 December and the following night, and was still engaged next day. At that time a small force of British troops arrived and managed to arrange a truce, during which Grivas could withdraw the anti-Communists into the centre of Athens, which was most likely to be held.

When the X people emerged from their houses, how-ever, the Communists broke the truce, and attacked again. Grivas and his men (and their wives and children) hastily took refuge in the police station and surrounding buildings, which stand one block further down the hill from Thyssion Square. There they were besieged by the E.L.A.S. troops, who now began to close in hard, until soon there was hand-to-hand fighting in several of the defended buildings, and it was quite certain that, if no aid arrived, Grivas and X would be wiped out altogether in about a couple of hours.

However, aid did arrive. The small British force returned and realized at once that, if the fight continued much longer, there would be a massacre. The British therefore forced the E.L.A.S. troops to cease fire, and they got the X-ists and their families away, many of them in lorries, to the Old Palace in the middle of Athens, where they found refuge. Grivas, his wife, and his wife's family were all thus rescued by British troops from almost certain slaughter. And they played very little further part in the operations which, once the British were rein-forced from Italy, succeeded in defeating the Communist rebellion by the middle of January.

Members of the X organization now claim that it

became thenceforth solely a political right-wing party, and had no responsibility for the assassinations and reprisals against Communists which followed the quashing of the rebellion—the white terror that succeeded the red. In Athens, indeed, where X were disarmed, this may largely have been so. But the symbol of X, with Grivas as its leader, now assumed much greater importance. The Communists had carried out their rebellion, whenever they were out of range of British troops, with such brutality and ferocity that most ordinary Greeks of no particular leaning to the right were ready to encourage anything that could avenge the horrors and protect the average citizens from their repetition. The Communist forces, unopposed by force anywhere outside Athens, had murdered and pillaged with almost unbelievable savagery. In Attica and the Peloponnese alone the bodies were found of 8,752 hostages who had been taken from towns and villages by E.L.A.S. and slaughtered. The total of those who lost their lives in this way is said to have been very much higher. Sickened by such massacres, longing to see them revenged, and above all terrified lest they should recur, the ordinary Greeks welcomed wandering groups of armed bandits who prowled through the countryside, hunting out stray Communists for slaughter in their turn, and attacking left-wing areas. These marauders mostly styled themselves as X-ists, though how closely they were in touch with Grivas, or whether they were in any way under his command, is somewhat doubtful. What can be said is that he made no attempt to repudiate them at that time, but welcomed the rapidly growing strength of royalist, right-wing sentiment, as well as the enrolment of many more ex-officers, which concentrated on the symbol of X and on the name of Colonel Grivas. The worst of the reprisal incidents occurred in the Peloponnese towards the end of January 1946, when a group of right-wing bandits, calling themselves X, and under the command of a Colonel Manganas, seized the town of Kalamata and held it for several days. At this town, some time before, the Communists had committed some horrible atrocities. When the right-wing band was forced out of Kalamata, it seized a number of hostages and withdrew into the hills. The Government was sufficiently aroused to proclaim martial law and to force the marauders to quit, but not before they had murdered some fifteen of the hostages. Apologists in Athens for the right-wing action now claim that Grivas had nothing to do with this raid on Kalamata, and that the symbol of X was taken in vain. But Grivas did not at the time repudiate it. Incidents of this kind were reinforcing his growing political influence, and, still more, his influence in the Army, where more and more senior officers were coming to his viewpoint, and where he gained control of the League of Young Officers.

This particularly gratified Grivas, since he himself had been retired from the Army with the rank, and rather meagre pension, of lieutenant-colonel in March 1945. The reason he was sacked is not in doubt—he was too embroiled in politics of the extreme right, and his name too firmly established as the symbol of right-wing thuggery. Senior officers were astonished, however, that he was no longer allowed to continue in his career. One of them, now one of the leading soldiers of Greece, says openly, 'We thought of him as the future Commander-in-Chief.' Grivas himself nursed a smouldering grievance at the politicians of Athens for affronting him, as indeed

they had. To make the fact quite plain, no acknowledge-
ment was made of his services during the campaign
against the Italians in Albania, and he did not receive any
decorations. At first he could console himself by the fear
linked with his name as the armed bands labelled X
carried on their white terror in the Peloponnese, and to
some extent in Thessally, and by the political influence he
could wield as a result. But even this waned. Once the
first post-war election had been held in March 1946, in
all the hubbub of shrieking propaganda, but watched
by observer teams from Britain and America, Grivas's
thunder was to some degree stolen. The Government put
into power was royalist, and it soon persuaded the British
to agree to bringing forward the plebiscite as to whether
the King should return to his throne. It was to have been
held in 1948; instead, it was now to take place in September 1946. In a flush of confidence, the Government started
to take action against extremes of both left and right.
Some of the left-wing leaders were exiled. The provincial
offices of Grivas's X organization were shut down, and
the leaders of some of the wandering armed bands
arrested. Grivas himself was not touched, but it must
have been clear to him that his political chances were
passing. When he stood at the 1950 elections as an X
Party candidate, he lost. He tried once again as a Populist
Party candidate. He was again a dismal failure.

His Army career was at an end, because of his political
ambitions. In politics he had had no success. Most ordinary people who had welcomed X just after the liberation,
as a counter-measure to the appalling atrocities committed by the Communists, now wearied of the senseless-
ness of vendettas and raids, so that the organization
itself no longer meant nearly as much as it had. Moreover,

it was too trivial to play any part in the real struggle with the Communists that was soon to come—the civil war in the north of Greece, in which the Communists were reinforced from across their northern frontiers. This was no guerrilla affair, but by 1946-7 had grown into full-scale war. The Communists were now met by the reconstituted Greek Army, five divisions of which were engaged. In 1949 General Papagos, who had commanded the Greek campaign in Albania, was appointed Commander-in-Chief; he had returned to Greece at the end of World War II from the concentration camp at Dachau into which the Germans had thrust him. He was successful in bringing to a conclusion by the end of that year a bitter struggle which had cost tens of thousands of lives, had turned one Greek in every ten into a refugee, had further dislocated the agriculture and industry of an already chaotic economy, and in which the Communists had outraged the opinion of the world by abducting about 25,000 Greek children across the border into Communist countries, where they were held as hostages.

In none of these events did Grivas take any part. What, then, was this failed soldier, failed politician doing? Unlike many retired lieutenant-colonels, Grivas did not play golf. Except when he was trying to promote his political party, he retired to his shabby flat at Thyssion, where his wife kept house and gossiped with her relatives. And there Grivas began an intensive course of study.

CHAPTER V

WHAT THE retired lieutenant-colonel was studying in his flat in Thyssion for five years after his
dismissal from the Army was the subject of power. His
craving for it had been sharpened by the series of disappointments he had suffered. He now intended to make
a careful study of the methods of the Communists, who
had nearly attained power in Greece, and would certainly
have done so had not British troops intervened in
December 1944. Where Grivas himself had failed, the
Communists had almost succeeded; throughout most of
this period, it looked in fact as though they still might,
and perhaps a Communist government might be established in Greece that would have to be fought by its own
guerrilla methods.

For five years, therefore, in his flat at Thyssion, Grivas
undertook a detailed study of the Communist organization and guerrilla forces in Greece. Being a trained staff
officer, he made his study systematically, slowly, with
great care. He noted in detail how the Communists had
worked through E.A.M. and E.L.A.S., and particularly
through their youth organization, not only in Athens, but
also in the mountains. Much of his careful enquiry and
investigation was concerned with details of organization
—how to hide, how to operate a messenger service that
will not betray its headquarters, how to apply ruthless
pressure to a civil population that is merely quiescent,

and so on. Much of his study was of the supply and concealment of weapons and explosives. And some of it was
theoretical. Before long he realized that there was one
basic proposition upon which the whole Communist
underground movement depended. It was that the first
step is to get hold of the young, and to turn them into
fanatics. A political terrorist organization that does this
is virtually impregnable. It has a reservoir, which is
always being filled by younger children still, from which
it can draw ceaselessly the personnel it needs for any task
from painting a slogan on a wall to political assassination.
The Communists had adopted this method; nearly all of
their gunmen in Athens were lads in their late teens or
early twenties, who prowled the streets assassinating
prominent men, officers, or any who could stand in the
way of the Communist progress, simply because they
were ordered to do so. One of these boys when interro-
gated in a police station when he was at last caught was
found to have murdered twenty people. He was asked
what he knew about any of them: he knew nothing except
that he had been told to shoot them. This was the basic
principle of the study of successful underground terrorism
that Grivas made in his otherwise idle years after 1945.

It is possible that, at first, he was preparing to equip
his X organization to go underground and fight if the
Communists should take Greece. But towards the end of
the '40s it became more and more sure that they would
not be permitted to. For not only were the Greek forces
making headway—and swift headway once General, later
Field-Marshal, Papagos took command—but the British
influence in Greece had been replaced by American.
From March 1947, when the Truman Doctrine made
available for Greece and Turkey the sum of 400 million

dollars, of which three-quarters would go to Greece, it was evident that the Americans had at last woken up to the danger of the Eastern Mediterranean falling to Soviet Russia. From that time onwards, it was unlikely that Grivas would have to apply, on the Greek mainland, the lesson he had learned so thoroughly.

But that did not necessarily mean that, once again, his lust for power would be frustrated. For a century and a half the Greeks had striven to bring into their national rule those territories abroad where lived large Greek populations. Anybody who could in this way add to Greater Greece would be assured of all the honour, respect and, if he so wished, power that the Greeks could lavish on him. Grivas therefore determined to apply his study to one such territory outside the frontiers of Greece. There were two that he chiefly considered. One was Northern Epirus, as the Greeks call it, or Southern Albania, as the Albanians, in whose territory it now rests, prefer to name it. There he would run against Soviet ruthlessness. The other was the island of Cyprus under the benign, rather soft rule of the British.

Grivas sat down and worked out a plan for winning Cyprus back to Greece by the methods of underground terrorism he had learned from a study of Communist tactics. This does not mean that he vaguely considered how he would set about the task if the opportunity should arise. He made a definite plan, which he worked out in detail on paper, as a staff officer and a former lecturer in military tactics would.

In the spring of 1959, when he had returned from Cyprus to Athens, he produced this plan he had written in 1950, and handed it to Lieut.-Colonel Homer Papadopoulos, who had been seconded from his duties in the Greek Army to act as General Grivas's aide-de-camp. Grivas said to Papadopoulos: 'You are a colonel. You are trained in military theory. Read this plan, and tell me whether I departed from it in Cyprus.'

Papadopoulos read the plan. When he returned it to Grivas he could reply: 'The plan was carried out to the letter. You did not depart from it at all.'

It is one thing, however, to make a plan, and yet another to find the backing for it and the opportunity to put it into operation. To discover how this was done, it is now necessary to leave Grivas for a while, in 1950, with his plan for terror in Cyprus neatly on paper, and to consider some other characters.

Most of them came originally from small villages in the island of Cyprus, lying only forty miles from the coast of Turkey, but inhabited mostly by Greeks—some 80 per cent. of the population of just over half a million. The Turks comprise only about 18 per cent. It is one of the loveliest and most fertile of the Mediterranean islands, and, under British rule, the most prosperous. It is always referred to as a small island, so that one thinks in terms of the Isle of Wight. In fact it covers 3,572 square miles, and is roughly the area of Kent, Surrey and Sussex.

The island is shaped rather like a frying-pan, with the long, narrow peninsula running off to the east, known by the troops as the Panhandle. The remainder of it is divided into three parts. Along the north coast, rising spectacularly almost from the sea to a height of 3,000 feet, is the narrow range of the Kyrenia Mountains, beneath which nestle a few coastal villages and the small and ancient port, and now holiday resort, of Kyrenia itself.

The central part of the island, in the middle of which sits Nicosia, the chief town, is a flat plain of cornfields dotted with small villages, some of them Greek, some Turkish, and some with mixed populations. On the eastern coast of this plain lies one of the two main ports of the island, Famagusta.

In the southern part of the island stand the Troodos Mountains, which rise through a tangled, thickly wooded range of precipitous heights, ridges and peaks to Mount Olympus at 6,401 feet. On the southern slopes of the Troodos Mountains and in the foothills which reach almost down to the coast and the other main port of Limassol, are spread the Cyprus vineyards. Into the hills above them pierce deep valleys, at the bottom of which meander small rivers through beds of grey shale. The good mountain roads twist steeply upwards in series of sharp hairpin bends, and on either side are scattered small villages or summer villas, and on the fertile ledges the peasant families cultivate their patches of ground. Here and there are shepherds with small flocks of sheep, and at almost every bend an old woman on a donkey, or a young girl herding a few goats, against a background of a steeply precipitous mountainside thickly covered with trees and vegetation, down which occasional water-falls tumble. Around the villages of the middle slopes cluster orchards where grow the most delicious apples and cherries. Higher still stand the little mountain holiday resorts, where there are comfortable hotels for the skiers in the winter, and for the wives and families in summer avoiding the very great heat of the plain. Here too, high up, are established some of the monasteries which dominate the Cyprus scene; at the western end of the range is the Kykko Monastery, and at the eastern the Makheras Monastery, both of them important to this story. On the highest ridges and peaks the vegetation is mainly pine trees, which are crowded into thick forests, and the scent of which hangs heavily on the rarefied air. Up here, too, are the mines where chrome and asbestos are hewn out of the mountains. In the summer months the thick woods of the intricately tangled ranges are full of birdsong; lower down, the houses are overgrown with bougainvillaea, and their gardens glow with a profusion of flowers.

This delectable island, after having been governed by the Lusignans and the Venetians, came under Turkish rule in 1571, and the Turks governed it until 1878, when they allowed the British to occupy and administer it in return for a promise to defend Turkey against Russian aggression. The British took it on, in fact, as a military base. When, in 1914, Turkey went to war with Britain, the British annexed the island of Cyprus, and in 1925 it became a Crown colony.

From almost the start of the British occupation there was agitation for Enosis—union with Greece—fostered largely by the Greek Orthodox Church in Cyprus. The Greek Church has always kept nationalism and national culture alive in areas where Greeks are under a foreign rule. Nothing very much happened, however, until 1929, when a Cypriot Greek delegation visited London praying that the island should be ceded to Greece. The Colonial Secretary replied rather stiffly that the request would not be granted, the subject was definitely closed, and further discussion would be unprofitable. Disgruntled, the delegation returned to Cyprus and a certain amount of agitation was made there. A couple of years later, in 1931, a measure was brought in to limit the use of schools for nationalist propaganda and taxes were increased in the budget. In September the

Cypriot Greek National Movement called on all Cypriot people to refuse to pay the taxes and to boycott British goods. In October the Bishop of Kitium, one of the three island bishops, resigned from the Legislative Council, and this was the signal for a protest demonstration outside Government House, where the then Governor, Sir Ronald Storrs, was having dinner. Some youths began to throw stones. Several police cars rushed up. One was overturned and set on fire. Somebody picked up a burning brand and threw it at Government House, which was then an old building largely of wooden construction. It was burned to the ground. Trouble arose all over the island. Warships and troops arrived from Egypt. The rising was put down in a week with about eight rebel casualties. Nicosia was fined £20,000 to pay for the damage. The Legislative Council was abolished. There was a great outcry in Greece, which Venizelos calmed. And the Cypriot ringleaders, including two of the bishops, were exiled to England, where they were established in a boarding-house in Bayswater, London.

One of the exiles, a young politician and lawyer named Savvas Loizides, had had the forethought, when he was arrested in Cyprus, to put his passport into his pocket and the police had been careless enough to let him retain it. One day, therefore, he announced in the Bayswater boarding-house that he was going to Liverpool, but went instead to Calais, and thence to Paris, where he wrote an open letter to the Cypriot newspapers. Then he went on to Athens, where he set up a little office in the Greek Cypriot cause and called it the National Office of Cyprus. With the help of the exiled Bishop of Kyrenia, who also got out of Bayswater a little later, he made a lot of propaganda until 1936, when Metaxas became Greek dictator and told Savvas Loizides to keep quiet. There was no time for Cypriot propaganda during the world war; Savvas Loizides was busy indeed, defending Greeks in the courts martial of the German occupation, where he was allowed to practise his profession. Not until 1947 was there again in Athens an office devoted to Cypriot matters. This time it was the Athens office of the Ethnarchy Council of Cyprus (a council of political advisers to the Archbishop). Savvas Loizides was one of the original members of the Council, and he became one of the people sitting in Athens who now enter the story. He is a short, tubby, smiling man with grey hair, grey moustache and a soft voice, and he smokes perpetually a pipe with a long stem, and is happy to discuss his hobby of sketching in water-colour. Several of his rather charming sketches of Athenian scenes adorn the walls of his legal office which he shares with his younger brother, Sokratis Loizides. Sokratis is a thickset man with a lot of black hair, who wears heavy horn-rimmed spectacles and who has spent some time in Wormwood Scrubs and Maidstone prisons on account of his adventures in Cyprus.

These two lawyers, the Loizides brothers, were typical of a small group of people of Cypriot birth, living in Athens, who from 1947 onwards were planning to revive an active campaign for the union of Cyprus with Greece. They were either members of, or were linked with, the Ethnarchy Council, and thus with the Church in Cyprus. The Archbishop in those years was Makarios II— Makarios is an ecclesiastical, not a family name. Waiting in the wings was one of the principal actors in the tragic story to follow, Michael Mouskos, a young priest who in 1948 had been enthroned as Bishop of Kitium, taking the name of Makarios and who, on the death of the then Archbishop in 1950, was to succeed him as Makarios III. This Makarios—the one who matters—had also spent the war years in Athens under the German occupation. He had been deacon of the St. Irini Church, and had already got to know George Grivas and his X organization. After the war he was in collaboration with the group of Cypriots in exile and irredentist Greeks who were contemplating a campaign of violence in the island. Among them was the Athenian lawyer, Zafiris Valvis, who had been an associate of Grivas in the X organization, and was said to have taken his beach-head plan to Cairo. Savvas Loizides insists that these people were not the Ethnarchy Council. But the Council must have known what was going on, just as Makarios did.

The group of plotters was really split into two groups —one party which wanted only passive resistance and sabotage, and one which was prepared to go the whole way with personal violence. To them was introduced the retired colonel, Grivas, with his careful staff plan. They asked him whether he favoured passive resistance and sabotage or terrorism. He replied that he favoured both, one after the other. The more pacific party then left the group. The others began to make ready to go ahead.

At this point the new Archbishop Makarios entered into the Grivas plan, virtually took command of it, undertook at any rate part of the financial backing it would require, and in 1951 invited Grivas to Cyprus to put the first part of it into action. What must be stressed is that his visit to Cyprus in that year at the invitation of Makarios was not fortuitous. It was already the plan for Cyprus terrorism being put into effect, quite deliberately and carefully.

The personal responsibility of Archbishop Makarios for the terrorism in Cyprus has been established beyond any doubt. This young and ambitious priest, with his long and serious face, precisely calm speech and imperturbable manner, had devoted himself to the cause of Enosis; to this he brought more vigour than his predecessors had shown, but the line he pursued had already been laid down by them. The first attempt by the British after the Second World War to plan greater democratic freedom for Cyprus was made by the Labour Government in 1946, which proposed a ten-year development plan, the return of the 1931 exiles, and the framing of a Constitution. It was rejected by the Ethnarchy Council, and by Leontios, the Bishop of Paphos, who was soon to be elected the first post-war Archbishop of the island. They refused to consider anything short of the union of Cyprus with Greece, and they bitterly opposed the constitutional plans which would remove political leadership from the Church and would probably end for ever the dream of Enosis.

Leontios died shortly after his election, and was succeeded by one of the bishops who had been exiled in 1931, the Bishop of Kyrenia. He became Archbishop Makarios II. In 1948 the British Government put up proposals for a Constituent Assembly which would have granted virtual self-government to Cyprus in all domestic matters, and considerable freedom in external affairs. The proposals were rejected by the Church because they did not accord the only demand which would satisfy it, union with Greece. The action of the Greek Cypriots led to the dissolution of the Constituent Assembly. The Communists then began to urge that a plebiscite should be held under the auspices of the United

Nations to reveal the strength of Cypriot desire for Enosis. Makarios II was trying to free himself from contact with the Communists, but on this occasion he was forced to accept their collaboration, and, conveniently forgetting all about the United Nations, to organize the plebiscite within the framework of the Church. The Bishop of Kitium—who was later to become Makarios III—took a large part in running this plebiscite, which was conducted in a somewhat unusual way. In January 1950 all Greek Cypriots were required to go to their churches and to sign publicly for or against Enosis; a negative vote could carry with it a threat of excommunication. It is not surprising that the plebiscite revealed an almost overwhelming desire among Greek Cypriots to be united with Greece.

It is certain that this desire existed in a rather mild form in most of the Greek Cypriots of the island. But few of them were sufficiently enthusiastic to take any action, and many had an uneasy feeling that it would be unwise to disturb the prosperity in which they lived under a benign British rule, or to exchange it for the poverty-stricken turbulence of Greece, which had only just emerged from a long and painful civil war. Moreover, the British rule did not in the least inhibit their Greek way of life. Their children followed in their schools the same curriculum as in Greek schools. They were taught in the Greek language by teachers who were freely permitted to advocate, as part of the lessons, the idea that Cyprus should be delivered from British rule. Although the Government is responsible for all elementary education, the teachers are, by law, of the Greek Orthodox religion, and the textbooks can refer to the slavery of the Greek people of Cyprus. In the Greek secondary schools, most of which are not provided by the Government, but by local committees, the pupils take a form of study which enables them to proceed to universities in Greece, just as readily as though they were citizens of that country. Greek Cypriot youths were allowed to enrol in the Greek Army and still retain their British nationality. There was no oppression of the Greek population, and the sole reason they did not enjoy a much wider measure of self-government was that their own Church forbade it.

But in spite of these material considerations, and the fear that should British rule be withdrawn Cyprus might fall under a Communist régime, it is still true that most Greek Cypriots were automatically in favour of union with Greece at some time or other (perhaps not very soon).

Makarios III was elected Archbishop in 1950, and was as denunciatory as any of his predecessors of the offers which the British Government held out of a freer and more democratic life for the Cypriots. What he said was, as an example: 'We want Enosis. We shall never lower the Enosis flag. We shall carry on the struggle uncompromisingly.'

This sort of language was what was expected from the Archbishops. But Makarios not only spoke it; he meant it and was already taking steps to translate it into vigorous and, if necessary, violent action. The first, which possibly he had discussed with Grivas when they met in Athens in 1949, was to secure a firmer grip on the young people of Cyprus through their religious clubs and organizations. There were a number of these which had been started after the war to provide religious teaching in opposition to the then very active Communist propaganda on the island. The chief of these organizations was known with the Greek love of initials, as O.H.E.N. (Orthodox Christian Union of Youth). At the head of it, Makarios placed one of the most fanatical Greek priests in Cyprus, Papastravos Papa Agathangelou, who promptly included in religious instruction such subjects as hatred of Britain and, later, sabotage.

Makarios also formed a new youth organization of a political nature, which had, of course, the backing of the Church. This was the Pancyprian National Youth Organization—P.E.O.N. In 1951, soon after its foundation, Makarios invited Grivas to come from Athens to advise on its organization and development.

But this was only the ostensible reason for his visit. The conspirators had now firmly decided to attempt a campaign of terrorism in Cyprus, and had appointed Grivas to conduct it. When Archbishop Makarios invited him to come to Cyprus in 1951, it was to make a military reconnaissance, and to spy out the land.

CHAPTER VI

GRIVAS MADE a thorough reconnaissance of Cyprus on his first post-war visit in 1951. As he had left the island as a youth, his memory of it was not vivid, and he travelled every road and studied every town and village street in which he proposed to establish groups of assassins. He collected maps of all parts of the island and spent a long time exploring the mountains over which he might expect to have to fight guerrilla actions and where it would be essential to prepare in advance a large number of hideouts, since he very well knew that no guerrilla force he could recruit in Cyprus could ever hope to stand up to British troops in battle. In fact, he discovered, when the time came, that he had overestimated the capacity of the young Cypriots for this sort of fighting, and had imported such weapons as Bren guns which were of little use—the effort of getting them there was largely wasted, since what was chiefly needed was small arms and bombs.

This visit in 1951 was only his first reconnaissance. He came back the following year, this time bringing his wife with him, and continued to plot in great detail the campaign of sabotage, murder and propaganda he intended to wage in Cyprus. On this second reconnaissance visit he met a young man named Andreas Azinas, who, he at once saw, would be of great assistance to him. Azinas, for one thing, shared his political views; his elder brother had been killed in 1949 in the civil war in Greece against the Communists. Andreas Azinas, a short, slim, dark-haired young man who had been educated at Reading University, where he obtained his diploma in agriculture, was an employee, and was later to be Secretary, of an island association of farmers' clubs. This association was used as a convenient place in which to put active Enosists; Sokratis Loizides, the younger of the two lawyer brothers in Athens, had been its Secretary until 1950, when he made such a nuisance of himself that, as he was a Greek national by then, the Cyprus Government kicked him off the island and told him not to come back.

Andreas Azinas entered wholeheartedly into Grivas's plans, and aided him in his reconnaissance, not only on this, but on at least two later occasions when Grivas came illegally into the island under an assumed name. The last of these reconnaissance journeys was early in 1954, a few months before he finally came to the island to settle down to putting the terrorist plan into action. On this last reconnaissance he made a special study of the commissariat—the food supplies on which he and his guerrillas would be able to count. He came to the conclusion that since he would spend most of his time in remote mountain hideouts, food supplies would be very precarious. He might be able to expect some cold meat, cooked several days earlier, perhaps twice a week. But fortunately the mountains of Cyprus abound for many months of the year with fruit—apples, oranges, cherries, medlars, strawberries and so on. Most of the time there would be fruit to be had for the picking if a man could keep fit on it. When he returned to Athens, therefore, Grivas told his wife that he had a stomach ulcer and the doctor had placed him on a regimen of nothing but two pieces of fruit every hour and a plate of cold meat twice a week. With his characteristic thoroughness, he remained on that diet until the time came for him to sail for Cyprus and terrorism, and thus accustomed his digestive organs to the food they would for many months receive.

The ostensible reason for Grivas's visit to Cyprus in 1951 was, as has been said, to help organize the political youth movement, P.E.O.N., which Archbishop Makarios had founded. Grivas was too busy to undertake this task himself, but he gave clear instructions on how it was to be done, for it was of vital importance to his plan that he should have available a militant and fanatical youth movement from which he could later recruit, not only his messengers, his slogan-writers and his pamphlet-distributors, but also his saboteurs and his gunmen, just as the Communists had done so successfully in Greece, and as he had tried to do, with less success, in his X organization. Under his instruction then, P.E.O.N. was thus organized.

The immediate task was to organize it into a network of clubs all over the island, each of which was in effect a cell for subversion. For the clubs had, in addition to their façade of respectable political purposes, secret rules and oaths which, of course, are the kind of thing to appeal to schoolboys anywhere. Most of the members were either schoolboys in the upper forms of the secondary schools or youngsters of about the same age from working-class families who were already in jobs and who could demonstrate that they were not only anti-British, but anti-Communist. The work of indoctrinating the youngsters began, as it always does, by setting them first to distribute

George Grivas in the mountains of Cyprus—a photograph captured by the British during the pursuit in 1956.

The man who deliberately brought Grivas and terrorism to Cyprus was Archbishop Makarios III, who in the end, in Grivas's view, betrayed the cause for which they had struggled.

leaflets and political literature—thus giving them an actual, active share in the political aim—and then by getting them to paint slogans on the walls of public buildings and by the roadsides. Within a year these children were painting up such slogans as 'Greeks, Liberty is won with Blood'.

What made it easier to indoctrinate the children was that most of their school-teachers were themselves strong protagonists of the same cause; many of them were Greeks from Greece. Their priests, too, were preaching and teaching the same lesson. And most of their parents, while they were perhaps a little uneasy at the lengths to which the children were going, were not themselves opposed in theory to the cause itself. After all, Enosis was what all the Greeks wanted, and had said they wanted for scores of years. A good many parental fears must have been felt, however, when their children started daubing on walls such slogans as 'Death to Traitors', and taking part in demonstrations, notably in Paphos, which grew into riots at the time of the celebrations of the Coronation of Queen Elizabeth in 1953. The police had to be called in to break up the mobs of youngsters. As a result, P.E.O.N. was declared illegal, and was forced to go underground. The Government's wisdom in banning it is open to question, since its indoctrination activities were largely transferred to the religious clubs of O.H.E.N., and its more violent activities, which included helping to smuggle in a shipload of arms from Greece in 1953, continued under cover.

The arms shipment was a direct result of Grivas's visit to Cyprus in 1951. From that time onward, weapons and ammunition were brought into the island from Greece and Rhodes, often in small quantities which were easily smuggled, and were concealed against the time that they would be needed.

It would seem therefore that at any time from about 1952 onwards the Grivas plan for Cyprus could have been put into operation. The conspirators in Athens were cohesively linked with Makarios in Nicosia. Sufficient money was available to finance the plan; not a great deal was required. An experienced and ruthless guerrilla leader was free to enter the island and start the violence. A small supply of arms was already in place. A network of fanatical youths existed from whom the saboteurs and gunmen could be drawn. Most of the Cypriot population were in sympathy with the political aims of the plan and could be counted upon to some extent to back up the guerrillas, or at least not to betray them. And yet two more years were to pass before action really began. What was lacking?

The Grivas plan still needed the support of the Greek Government, which was still withheld.

In Greece itself, Field-Marshal Papagos had stepped into politics by forming a new party, the Greek Rally, to fight in the 1950 elections. Papagos, the greatest Greek figure thrown up by the war and by the civil war, was held in much the same sort of veneration in Greece that General de Gaulle commands in France, and the political methods he used were also similar to General de Gaulle's —notably an attack on the squabbles of the old parties. The elections of 1952 were a landslide in favour of Papagos, and the Field-Marshal came to the government of his country with the first large working majority that the Greek elections had provided since the war.

He used it effectively. Already a national hero from his defeat of Mussolini's invasion, and the saviour of the nation from the Communist assault in the north, he now acted vigorously to put the Greek economy into a more viable state, entered into a friendly pact with Jugoslavia and Turkey, resumed diplomatic relations with Russia, and soon afterwards permitted the United States to establish bases on Greek soil. If he could now bring at least one of the two major pockets of Greeks under foreign rule into the dominion of Greece herself, and thus fulfil one of the cherished dreams of all patriotic Greeks, it would be the crowning achievement of a wonderful career. It was unlikely, of course, that Albania, the Soviet satellite, would yield up the territory of Northern Epirus. But the Field-Marshal, who was badly advised on this point, genuinely thought that the British could be persuaded without much trouble peacefully and willingly to hand over Cyprus. Many Greeks held this view. They knew with what friendship the British regarded the Greeks. And it is true that on one occasion in 1915 Britain had actually offered Cyprus to Greece if she would enter the war on the side of the Allies. The Greeks would not and the offer was withdrawn. When, in the next world war, Greece fought willingly and gallantly on the side of Britain and suffered so much in doing so, many Greeks seemed to have assumed that the automatic reward, after the war, would be Cyprus. They were surprised, indeed, when Enosis was not granted, but was categorically ruled out of the question. It was understood that the British needed a military base in the Eastern Mediterranean, especially after the withdrawal of troops from Egypt, but Field-Marshal Papagos felt—with some reason—that a N.A.T.O. base would be just as effective and could as easily be provided under Greek as under British sovereignty. He decided to raise the question with

Britain, at first informally. But the occasion on which he chose to do so was an unhappy one. Mr. Anthony Eden came to Greece to recuperate after a severe illness. He was still far from recovered in health, but, of course, consented to a proposal that Field-Marshal Papagos and he should meet at dinner. On that social occasion Papagos tentatively raised the question of Cyprus, expecting, as he had been advised, a soft answer that might well lead to more formal negotiations at a later date. What he got instead was a tired, perhaps rather abrupt reply from Mr. Eden that he really could not be expected to discuss Cyprus on such an occasion. The Field-Marshal, who chose to take this as a deliberate snub, is said to have gone pale and silent with anger. And there seems little doubt that such a trivial happening had a marked effect on the attitude he adopted towards the whole question of the Enosis of Cyprus with Greece. He became readier to listen to the persuasions which were being whispered to him by Makarios and by other interested persons that the only course to follow in Cyprus was direct action. He also, during the last year of his life, was himself so ill that his personal judgement may well be regarded as impaired.

The Cypriot conspirators in Athens insist that, although the Greek Government may well have known that something was going on, it gave no active help; it merely refrained from hindering. But it is difficult to reconcile this with the facts—the most obvious of which is that Athens Radio directed at Cyprus a stream of propaganda which became more and more virulently anti-British, and on many occasions incited to violence. What the conspirators wanted from Papagos, and what indeed they expected to receive once the attack had been

68

launched, was the infiltration of Greek Army officers into Cyprus to help carry it on. But this they did not get.

In July 1954 the British Government made yet another attempt to introduce some form of representative government into Cyprus. It proposed to set up a Legislative Council which was considerably less liberal than that offered in 1948 and afterwards, in that it would have a majority of non-elected members; since the Greek Cypriot nationalists would not co-operate, anything more liberal might well have handed over the island to a Communist government.

Makarios at once rejected the modified Constitution. 'No one will wish', he declared, 'to forge the bonds of Cypriot slavery by co-operating with the ruler, thus becoming a shameful traitor to his country.' And from the pulpit he thundered: 'We shall consider as enemies of our national cause those who may give in to the Government's constitutional pressure. We shall brand such persons as traitors, and we shall be unable to protect them from the people's rage and shame.'

He pressed the Greek Government to take the matter to the United Nations, and himself went to New York in December of that year. But the move with the United Nations failed. Makarios came back through Athens and talked once again to the Field-Marshal, urging that he should now consent to direct action in Cyprus itself. There is no question but that, at this stage, Field-Marshal Papagos told Makarios to go ahead.

He was in a position to do so. Several months earlier, in August, he had called a private meeting at Mesapotamus Monastery of a number of people who were determined on Enosis with Greece. Also there was Zafiris Valvis, the Athenian lawyer who had for long been

Grivas's associate. It was decided at that meeting to go ahead with the plan for sabotage and terrorism, and Valvis was given the special job of organizing the supply of arms and explosives from Greece.

Moreover, Makarios was ready to start because, by the time he met Papagos in Athens, his chief terrorist was already in position in Cyprus. Grivas was there.

During October, in his flat at Thyssion in Athens, he had looked out his old military boots and told his wife that she had better give them away; he would not be using them any more. Before she could do so, however, he pretended to change his mind. After all, he said, they were mementoes of his fighting days, so perhaps after all he would keep them as souvenirs. But he deplored the state into which they had fallen and told his wife to take them round to the cobbler and get them properly repaired before he put them away again.

Later in the month, on 26 October 1954, he left the house without mentioning to his wife that he was going anywhere in particular. For all she knew, he was merely walking down to the coffee-shop for an hour or so, or intended to take a stroll in the gardens below the Acropolis. But the day wore on, and he did not come back. He still had not returned by nightfall. Kiki, his wife, was not in the least perturbed by this. For her, whatever her husband did was right, and she did not expect to be told or consulted about his plans. If she happened to look around the flat, she might have been slightly worried to discover that not only her husband, but also his military boots had gone. A couple of days later a friend came surreptitiously and whispered to her something of what had happened.

What had in fact happened was that George Grivas,

accompanied by Sokratis, the younger of the two Loizides brothers, had taken ship for Rhodes. They arrived there at three o'clock the following afternoon. It was pouring with rain. From there they intended to travel secretly and illegally to Cyprus in a fishing boat; Grivas's earlier application for legal entry had been refused, and Sokratis Loizides was still a banned person.

They expected to set out for Cyprus the next day (it was still raining heavily), but the departure was postponed. Grivas made use of the delay to organize a centre in Rhodes from which arms could be shipped, and made arrangements for the next delivery of a *caique*-load. The delay, and the filthy weather, were getting on his nerves badly, and he confided to his diary such remarks as 'Agony!' But on 6 November the fishing boat came into harbour, was refuelled, and made ready for the departure during the night of the following day.

After dark on 7 November Grivas and Loizides slipped quietly aboard the *caique* in Callithea Bay, and she finally got under way at a quarter of an hour past midnight. The weather had cheered up a little, and Grivas, who is a very poor sailor, felt relieved. But he rejoiced too soon. On 9 November, as they sailed towards Cyprus, a fierce storm blew up.

'The waves were so enormous', says Sokratis Loizides, 'that several times I thought the ship would sink. I was perhaps more frightened than I need have been because I know very little of nautical matters. In addition to being frightened by the storm, I was also rather sea-sick. But I was not nearly as sea-sick as the Leader. He looked terrible. He lay in the boat with his eyes closed, as white as a sheet, and seemed to be unconscious.'

At ten o'clock that night the fishing boat arrived off

the west coast of Cyprus, at a quiet bay not far from Paphos. Grivas was assisted ashore on to the beach, where several men were waiting to receive him. He was taken, exhausted, to a house in the village of Khlorakas. The sombre drama of the next four years in Cyprus could no longer be avoided except with the consent of Archbishop Makarios and George Grivas, who promised to lay down his arms when the Archbishop instructed him to do so, but not before. The terrorist had arrived.

CHAPTER VII

IT IS ASTONISHING that although the British authorities in Cyprus knew quite a lot of what was going on, they did so little to counter it that Grivas was able, for at least six months after his clandestine arrival, to travel openly about the island, taking few precautions to conceal himself.

There is no doubt that the authorities did know that something was going on. Towards the end of October the police received reports that arms and saboteurs had been shipped from Greece into the island, and in the following month they had definite information that a Greek Army officer had landed secretly and was organizing and training saboteurs. They did not as yet know who he was, but they had found that out too by the end of the month; or, at any rate, they had been told by an informant whom they did not know whether or not to trust, though his information was in fact accurate. In spite of this knowledge, and of the dangerous situation which was clearly building up, the police gave Grivas little or no trouble in those early months. He was living at first mostly with young Azinas—the Reading University student who had become Secretary for the association of farmers' clubs. They stayed in several houses in and around Greater Nicosia. Nicosia itself is a centuries-old walled town, surrounded by an empty moat, across which are pierced several exits by way of gates in the wall. Within the wall itself is the old city, a confused warren of narrow, straggling streets; even Ledra Street, where the chief shops are, would rate as a back-street in most small towns. Here, one would have thought, was the ideal place for a man to hide. But Grivas did not think like that. He believed that the best place to hide was not the obvious, but the most unlikely. The houses in which he and Azinas stayed, therefore, were all outside the wall in the more modern and prosperous districts, where the roads are wider and the people far less crowded. There was one house in which they stayed near the outlying suburb of Strovolos, close to Government House and the Government Secretariat. There were other houses closer in to Nicosia itself—outside the Famagusta Gate, for example, and in the small Greek section set in the Turkish and Armenian quarter outside the Kyrenia Gate. In these houses Grivas stayed during his first weeks in Cyprus, and in one of them he started to have a cellar dug out beneath the floor, paved with concrete and entered through a hidden trap-door.

He did not, however, spend much of his time in these houses, for he, Sokratis Loizides, and Andreas Azinas were busy getting together the organization which he was later to suggest to the Archbishop should be called E.O.K.A. (the Greek initials of National Organization of Cypriot Combatants), together with its ancillary organizations. This meant travelling all over the island, for although Loizides, with his past contacts through the farmers' clubs, and Azinas in his present capacity could go through all the villages, recommending likely local leaders, Grivas would appoint no one until he had met him personally, and studied and assessed him. Most hours of the day were therefore spent travelling by car from place to place meeting local candidates for the underground organization. Grivas would sometimes stick at this work for more than twenty hours a day. After returning to the house in which he was currently staying, and getting to bed at, say four o'clock in the morning, he was up at six, rousing Azinas, who was exhausted after an equally vigorous day, and compelling him to start on the course of physical exercises with which Grivas invariably began his day and in which he insisted the others should join; when all the rest had stopped from fatigue, Grivas was exercising steadily on. Then he ate a couple of oranges and set out on the next day's work, quite openly, by car. It was during this period, indeed, that while he was making a reconnaissance of the military installations at Episkopi, his car stuck in the mud of a roadside ditch and he could not get it out. A British Army lorry came along full of troops and he signalled to the driver to stop, explaining with gestures the obvious plight he was in; Grivas speaks very little English. The lorry-driver good-naturedly got out a tow-rope and hauled Grivas's car from the mud, then the British troops went on their way smiling benignly as Grivas waved his thanks.

This trivial example illustrates with what laxity the security of the island was at that time being safeguarded. The first sabotage blow with explosives was not to take place until 1 April of the following year. Not only until that date, but even for a short time after it, Grivas was able to circulate in the island with sufficient freedom to construct his E.O.K.A. organization, train the men he had chosen and keep in touch with his fellow conspirators in Athens; the authorities did not seem to have had their suspicions aroused in the slightest when Azinas travelled back and forth by air between Nicosia and Athens, where he was arranging with Greek agents the purchase and transhipment of arms.

Before describing the organization which Grivas set up, it is necessary to enquire exactly what its purpose was.

Its first aim was to influence world opinion. Primarily, the battle of Cyprus was a propaganda battle. Neither Grivas, Makarios, the sponsors of E.O.K.A., nor the members of the Greek Government who had consented to the plan, imagined that the British could be driven from the island by force; although there was at one time a fear that Grivas could rouse the whole Greek population of Cyprus into rebellion, such a step was never really contemplated. What it was hoped to do was so to persuade public opinion, internationally, and in Britain itself, that Cyprus was being oppressed, that the British Government would finally be pushed into giving up the colony to Greece.

There was already some material to hand, and the more sober of the conspirators hoped that this could be achieved peacefully and that the process would begin at the meeting of the United Nations Assembly in December 1954. This was a hope that Grivas himself regarded with scorn. In his opinion, the United Nations would do nothing, especially as the United States was, on this topic, favourable to the British view. In the event he was right; the United Nations refused to discuss the problem of Cyprus and Makarios came flying home from New York, stopping on the way to talk to Field-Marshal Papagos.

In Grivas's view there would be no international action in favour of Greece until it could be shown that the Cypriots themselves were engaged in an active armed insurrection against British rule. This is what would convince world opinion, and indeed radical opinion in Britain, that the people of Cyprus were being denied freedom of self-determination—as, in fact, they were. At that early stage before the Turks grew vociferous too, the arguments against allowing the Cypriots to manage their own affairs were quibbling, biassed by a fear of a Communist success in the island, and, except where they were military, unworthy. Makarios and Grivas had this national basis for their campaign, although upon it they built a structure of assassination, violence and terror.

The basic reason for conducting a campaign of terror was not, therefore, to attack the British, but to arouse the Greek population of the island into a bitter opposition to British rule; and that was the situation which the Greek Government would then exploit on the international level and in the United Nations. In order to arouse the general public of Cyprus to this state of feeling, terrorism was to be used in three successive stages.

The first was, by such acts of sabotage as blowing up a broadcasting transmitter or a police station, to show the Greek Cypriots that there was at last a force on the island which was determined to win for them the Enosis which they had so long, if rather half-heartedly, demanded. At the same time rioting and insubordination by the schoolchildren of the island, incited by their teachers and priests, would inflame in that island where the family is a most important unit, feelings of pride and patriotism in the parents of such ardent young boys and girls. These feelings were to be further played upon by a stream of propaganda leaflets from Grivas. Meanwhile, the vituperous broadcasts permitted by the Greek Government from Radio Athens would comfortingly assure the Cypriots that they were not alone in the struggle, but that the whole of Greece was also at their side.

The second stage of the plan was to assault and in some cases to murder those individual Greek Cypriots who either collaborated with the British—for example, policemen—or disagreed with the violent methods of E.O.K.A. From these acts of violence Grivas would draw a double dividend. He would minimize the risk of betrayal by killing known traitors and thus terrifying potential ones. And he would frighten those ordinary Cypriots who were unenthusiastic or lukewarm about Enosis into expressing, and at last coming to feel, fervour for the cause. The terror would also assist in raising such funds as might be required. At the same time, by selecting his gunmen from the youngsters of the island, he ensured that any who were caught would command such tremendous sympathy that they would soon be transformed into national heroes and martyrs. E.O.K.A. leaflets that would pour in a violent outfall from his pen would still further harrow the feelings of the public. And he could rely on Athens Radio to contribute more than its share. With every incident, every week that passed, the propaganda picture would be built up of a small, heroic population striving for freedom from a rule that was, necessarily, becoming ever more oppressive, while the very children fought for their motherland: and thus the Greek Government would be provided with ever more inflammable material to carry time and again to the forum of the United Nations.

The third stage in the plan was to murder British troops and, later, civilians. This would be bound to provoke disciplinary and repressive measures of self-protection which would finally antagonize the whole Cypriot Greek population and weld it into so implacable an enemy of British rule that the shrieks of propaganda must assuredly be heard in New York, and the British would at last be compelled to yield to the censure of an outraged world opinion.

That was the plan.

To carry it out there was one basic necessity—to keep in being a hard core of gunmen and saboteurs under Grivas's own command who would continue to commit sporadic acts of assassination and violence, no matter how long the campaign lasted. That was what really mattered. Everything else would follow from that. Provided the violence and the inevitable counter-measures continued, there would always be plenty of propagandists, of willing helpers, and of enraged supporters. The hard core need not be large. At first it numbered fewer than forty young men of whom only a handful were determined assassins. At its peak E.O.K.A. had no more than about 300 terrorists—although, of course, it had thousands of more or less active supporters—and of those 300 probably not one in three could be relied on for anything more desperate than the hasty explosion of a distant bomb or a quick burst of fire in self-defence against attacking British troops.

The organization which Grivas set about creating in the last months of 1954 and the first of 1955 was fairly elaborate. At the top of the pyramid was himself, the Leader, together with a very small central headquarters. This headquarters was mobile and, so far as possible, invisible. Surrounding the headquarters were a few groups of guerrilla fighters, each band numbering between five and ten men and each led by a young man in whom Grivas had confidence; his confidence was on several occasions shattered. The guerrilla groups not only acted as a fence around the central headquarters and Grivas himself, but were also expected to carry out raids on British troops, road ambushes, and major sabotage operations.

The chief commanders of these groups were also the military commanders of the E.O.K.A. districts in which they were established. Under their orders came the local town and village gangs, which carried out lesser acts of sabotage, distribution of leaflets, and also assassinations. In each district the number of young men who were entrusted with the job of murder was, again, very small. Those who were given murders to commit were brought gradually to the pitch of shooting to kill through a long and testing training that began with smearing slogans on a wall and graduated through throwing bombs into an open window or a bar and running away. These killers were always extracted from the mob of young boys who, together with quite a number of girls, formed the bulk of the local gangs.

It is clear that an organization of this kind, with a hidden, secret leadership, could function only so long as its communications functioned. Grivas therefore devised a most elaborate and ingenious system of courier networks which, as will be seen, often broke down in operation, but never completely failed, and never betrayed the inmost secret of all, the whereabouts of Grivas himself.

Surrounding the E.O.K.A. organization was much more. There was a political organization called P.E.K.A., consisting mainly of teachers and priests, whose function it was to continue to indoctrinate the children and the village peasants. Eventually a special organization called

Schoolboys armed with sticks, stones and bottles line the walls of the Pancyprian Gymnasium in Nicosia, Cyprus's biggest school. It was from schoolchildren that Grivas recruited his couriers, his propagandists and, at last, his assassins.

Nicosia schoolgirls drag a sackload of empty bottles to hurl at British troops and police. The corruption of a whole generation of Cypriot children was part of Grivas's plan, modelled on Communist tactics.

The hideouts. Paratroops found this hole, hidden by a heap of straw, in a farmhouse wall, and caught six terrorists in the secret room behind it. The buildings of Cyprus were honeycombed with hundreds of such hides.

The hideouts. In a cavity measuring only 6 feet by 4 feet beneath false tiles in a bedroom floor in the village of Kato Dikhomo, Grivas's lieutenant, Matsis, was found and killed.

A.N.E. was formed as E.O.K.A.'s youth section to carry out rather more active functions, such as throwing stones through windows of shopkeepers who failed to obey the instruction to boycott British goods.

There was also, linked with P.E.K.A., but under the direct command of Grivas himself through the central headquarters, a Press and propaganda section which circulated E.O.K.A.'s news and pamphlets to newspaper offices and its more confidential orders to responsible members of E.O.K.A. itself.

In finding the men to set up this organization, Grivas soon discovered that he had to work with, on the whole, rather poor material. It was not that the Greek Cypriots were cowardly—that would be quite untrue. But they had lived so long in an atmosphere of calm that few of them had any real conception of vigorous action. There were also a few who gave other sorts of trouble, such as defaulting with payments to the grocer; Grivas turned them sharply out of his organization, regretting bitterly the fact that to execute them with his own hands would risk giving the whole game away.

For his most active men Grivas turned to the leaders of P.E.O.N., the youth organization which Archbishop Makarios had founded in 1950 and which the authorities had driven underground in 1953. The most valuable man he got from that source was a young clerk named Markos Drakos, who had been one of the five members of the Nicosia district committee of P.E.O.N. and was to become a leading terrorist in E.O.K.A. with a price of £5,000 on his head. But the man whom Grivas most trusted and who became his second in command was rather older. He was a twenty-six-year-old lorry-driver at Lysi named Gregorios Afxentiou, who had served in the

Greek Army from 1948 until 1952 before returning to Cyprus. He was still on the reserve of officers of the Greek Army, and he begged Grivas to assign to him some active role in E.O.K.A. Grivas was impressed from the first, not only by the man's apparent determination, but by the precision with which he carried out orders. But to test him out he first assigned him to sabotage work in the Famagusta area.

As Grivas organized his groups, and started to give the young men training in the use of weapons and explosives, he was also concerning himself with two chief worries: Would the international situation work to his advantage? And would they succeed in running into Cyprus a *caique*-load of explosives and arms that had been purchased and packed in Athens and were to be smuggled through in a fishing boat from Rhodes? Azinas received word from Athens that the load had left Greece towards the end of November.

CHAPTER VIII

THE ANSWER to his first problem was to come when Archbishop Makarios arrived back in Cyprus on 10 January 1955 from his journey to America. He had come via Athens, where he had consulted Field-Marshal Papagos.

The day after his return to Nicosia, Makarios summoned Grivas to the bishopric at Larnaca, where the Bishop of Kitium dwelt, and there they had their first meeting in Cyprus. Grivas kept a very full diary of this period, and it was later discovered and extracts were published by Her Majesty's Stationery Office, so that the story of this interview between the Archbishop and his strong-arm man is well known. In effect, the Archbishop said that Field-Marshal Papagos now wanted action, since the United Nations attempt had failed, and Grivas was to get on with it. The interview ended when a police car was seen outside the bishopric. The two prelates departed, and half an hour later Grivas and Azinas followed them, Azinas relating in detail what cash the Archbishop had put up in Athens to pay for the fishing boat and its load of arms.

The arrival of this fishing boat, the *St. George*, was badly bungled. Far too many people in Athens knew about it, and its sailing was too long delayed. Throughout December Grivas waited for news of it, and none came. In the new year there was still silence. But on 14

January 1955 Azinas came to see Grivas in the house just outside Nicosia where he was hiding and showed him a telegram from Athens announcing that the *caique* had sailed. Grivas and Azinas drove to Khlorakas later that day—the little coastal village near Paphos where Grivas and Sokratis Loizides had themselves landed—to make arrangements for the reception of the arms and to make sure that the police had not been alerted. All seemed well, and by driving fast they got back to Nicosia before midnight.

The following day came the alarm. Azinas sent a message to Grivas to come to him, since he had some vital news to impart. When they met, he told Grivas he had been to see the Archbishop, who had learned that the authorities knew a *caique* was on the way (though their information as to where it would arrive was not quite accurate). The Archbishop had this news because the cause of Enosis was well established among Greek Cypriots in official positions, not only in the Civil Service, but also in the police; E.O.K.A. rarely lacked accurate information about what the police knew.

Grivas was in a cold rage and spent the day trying to determine who the traitor could be who had given away the arrival of the *caique*. In fact, as he later learned, the betrayal had not come from Cyprus; it was simply that people had talked too much in Athens.

Azinas went back to the Paphos area, and a net of E.O.K.A. men was spread along the coast to watch for the *caique* and for the police. For a few days there was no sign of either. But on 17 January it became clear that the police were on the alert and the Army was co-operating with them. Special Branch policemen had come into the area and a radar watch was being kept. When Grivas received this news next morning he sent quickly to the Archbishop to tell him that a diversionary operation would be needed further round the coast at Xeros (where, as Grivas thought, the police really expected the *caique* to arrive), and to suggest that the Archbishop should send some of his own young men to carry out the diversion. But this Makarios refused to do, so Grivas had to detail a couple of his half-trained sabotage groups for the job.

Before long Azinas had come back to Nicosia from Paphos with fuller reports of police activity. There were patrols out along the stretch of coast where the fishing boat really was due to arrive, and a check was being made of all cars driving towards Limassol.

And still the ship did not arrive.

At this point Grivas took real alarm. There was nothing for it but to stop the present operation and bring the ship in later and elsewhere. So Azinas would have to fly to Athens to arrange this. Azinas was ready to go, but the Archbishop, nervous lest he himself should be implicated, delayed his departure for a couple of days before at last he agreed to the journey.

By then it was too late. Azinas was to fly first to Athens to find out how the betrayal of news had occurred, and then to Rhodes to give the skipper of the *caique* new sealed instructions to be opened only when he was just about to sail. But the *caique* *St. George* had already left and it arrived off-shore at the rendezvous after dark on 25 January.

At this point the police authorities in Cyprus at last tumbled to the fact that Azinas was mixed up in the plot that was preparing, and he became a wanted man. He therefore remained in Athens as the principal agent of

Grivas throughout the four years of terrorism, and of the Archbishop until he himself turned up in Athens when he was released from detention in the Seychelles Islands.

A reception party of eight E.O.K.A. men went down to unload the *St. George* as she lay off-shore just clear of the shallows. Leading them was Sokratis Loizides. He had been advised to stay away from the place because of the extent of the betrayal. But Sokratis was an unhappy man. He had recently married in Greece and his bride had raised hell because he had to leave her. He had already murmured to Azinas that he wished he had brought her with him to Cyprus; Grivas, when he heard of this, commented bitterly: 'Apparently he thought we were going to a wedding!' But Sokratis had reason for dismay. His wife was eventually to leave him, as he himself says, because of his revolutionary activities. This, of course, he did not know at that time. What he planned was to help unload the arms from the *St. George* and then sail in her back to Greece. So he eagerly led the party of eight out to the fishing boat and they climbed aboard and started to unload her.

On top of the cargo were several cases of small arms and ammunition which were either of Greek origin or had been packed in Greece. Below were stowed twenty-seven cases of explosives containing more than 10,000 sticks of dynamite, all of Greek origin and packed by the Hellenic Detonator and Explosives Company of Athens.

As the unloading began a strong force of police appeared and quickly cut off the *St. George*, her crew of five and the eight unloaders. Before they could be seized, the crew managed to slip overboard into the sea the cases of arms and ammunition, leaving on board only the dynamite, which they made some attempt of pretending was being smuggled in for fishing purposes. Some weeks later, however, a Marine diving team recovered the arms and ammunition from the sea bed and their evidence was held, at the trial of the crew and the E.O.K.A. unloaders, to be conclusive that these cases had also been on board the *St. George* when the police had arrived.

The immediate course, naturally, was to arrest all thirteen men and put them into Paphos Prison. It was on the evening of the following day that Grivas received the news; he had gone to an eastern suburb of Nicosia to meet Afxentiou, whose training was nearly completed and whom Grivas was going to entrust with a major job in his organization. Grivas was aghast at the tale of the fishing boat, the arrest of the men, and the loss of the arms and explosives. He poured out dramatic curses on whoever had given them away—he was, for a conspirator, always a very talkative man, and he spoke in highly charged terms, often emphasizing a point by a quotation from the classics, which were his favourite reading. He also sent an emotional message to the Archbishop that he would continue the struggle none the less.

But the capture of the arms ship had badly shaken Grivas, and he began for the first time seriously to worry about his own security. Although he was still in the Nicosia area, he knew that soon he would have to take to the mountains. He therefore pressed on with the job of forming the mountain gangs who would be grouped around to protect him and who were being recruited from the most promising of the sabotage trainees, many of them from Nicosia. To the district leaders in the mountain areas he sent instructions to make certain of safe houses that could be used in the villages, to organize groups that could manufacture home-made bombs, to assure the supply of food and stores, and to prepare to meet a British attack with guerrilla warfare. Grivas himself now to some extent restricted his movements. Although the police were still not bothering him, and he could move about Cyprus with fair freedom, he began to test his security plan of hiding-up far more closely in one or other of the houses he had chosen around Nicosia, accompanied only by two strong-arm men as bodyguard and reached by only one or two of his closest associates, nobody else knowing where he was. He began, also, to adopt his policy of remaining in one place for as long as possible and leaving it only when he had any suspicion that it might be compromised.

The most trivial suspicion, however, could send him darting nervously off into some other hiding-place. One of the oddest of these happenings occurred when he was established in an outbuilding of a house where lived a man and his wife and their four-year-old son. Only the man and his wife knew he was there and all messages were passed by devious routes to them. But one day the small boy asked his father: 'Where's the old grandad?' (He used a Greek word for 'grandfather', which does not imply relationship, but could almost be translated as 'the old man'.) The boy's father asked: 'What old grandad? Who do you mean?' The child replied, pointing at the outbuilding: 'The man who's hiding in there.'

Grivas, whose security had been breached by an infant when all the police could not find him, left hastily directly darkness fell that night. He did not tell the couple in the house where he was going and for a time he was cut off from contact with his organization—until he himself re-established it through another messenger.

At this earlier time, at the beginning of 1955, Grivas

left his hiding-place only to be taken to meet Makarios at the Kykko Monastery annexe, which stood just outside Nicosia, close to Government House, and in the area of the Government Secretariat. The purpose of these meetings was for Grivas to get from the Archbishop the money necessary to meet the expenses of the organization (about £200 a month); and for the purchases of explosives and arms as they were made available; and for Makarios to give Grivas instructions on the violent operations which were now soon to take place. The Archbishop's instructions were that the first attacks were to be made by sabotage of Government and military installations, but there were to be no casualties. Grivas pressed for permission to start what he called 'guerrilla activities' at the same time; by this he meant ambushing of military vehicles on lonely roads. But Makarios refused permission and Grivas had to comply. He was not yet in his impregnable mountain fastness from which he could, if he wished, defy any instructions provided he held around him the few hard-core E.O.K.A. fighters upon whom he could best rely. Indeed, he had not as yet many people upon whom he felt he could rely at all. The whole plan was in considerable chaos. The arms shipment had been bungled and the lieutenant he brought with him from Greece captured. The young men whom he had to turn into guerrillas and assassins had proved far from suitable for the task. An exception was Markos Drakos, one of the P.E.O.N. Committee, whom Grivas eventually made the district commander in Nicosia. But some of the others were lazy, some stupid, one or two were not above cheating the Leader in money matters, and nearly all of them lacked any sort of military training. Grivas moaned that he had to do everything himself, teach them, show them, build up a fighting machine from ill-adapted adolescents who were ardent in theory, but who shrank when it came to murder in practice. Once or twice he rounded on them suddenly and made it quite clear that he was not joking when he promised to shoot anyone who turned back or who disobeyed his orders. It would all be much easier for him when the violence had started and he could demonstrate to waverers by means of his young gunmen that he was in earnest.

To add to Grivas's irritation, Savvas Loizides—the elder lawyer brother in Athens—had written to the Archbishop protesting at the fiction, still being preserved, that the fishing boat had merely been smuggling dynamite for peaceful purposes. This made Sokratis out to be nothing but an ordinary smuggler. What Savvas wanted was a proud announcement that this act of unprecedented heroism, etc., would mark the beginning of a new struggle for freedom in Cyprus. The Archbishop thought that as the Cyprus Government knew the boat was also bringing in arms, there would be no harm in this. But at last Grivas persuaded him to wait until after the campaign of violence had actually begun; until then he insisted that every effort should be made to persuade the British that the capture of the boat had completely discouraged him and that all he intended was to get out of Cyprus as secretly and as soon as he could.

In one phase of his plan of action, however, Grivas was already having considerable success. This was among the schoolchildren. Grivas had turned to the older members of the underground youth movement, P.E.O.N., as a reservoir from which to draw his men of violence; in addition to Drakos, the former Secretary-General named Poskotis was engaged in training for sabotage only a few days after Grivas landed in Cyprus. The former Secretary in the Limassol district, Evghenios Cotsapas, son of an Ethnarchy councillor, was caught at about the same time carrying bombs in his car. And members of the Nicosia Committee were quickly enrolled as guerrilla fighters. It was from members of P.E.O.N. that he recruited most of his sabotage groups in the towns and the villages, distributing hand-grenades to them and keeping them under his direct military command, without interference from the priesthood.

Now he also stimulated the setting up of E.O.K.A. cells in the upper forms of the secondary schools, so that the mass of schoolchildren could be used for slogan-painting, leaflet distribution, and especially for mob demonstrations on special occasions, since a rioting crowd of schoolchildren was the most difficult type of mob for the police to handle without incurring accusations of brutality. In getting this organization into being, Grivas had the help of the priests and of some school-teachers—particularly those who were Greek nationals. But he depended more and more upon the elder boys themselves, who were established as group leaders within their classrooms, enrolling their fellow pupils and sending them along to the priests to have administered to them the E.O.K.A. oath:

'I swear in the name of the Holy Trinity that:

'(1) I shall work with all my power for the liberation of Cyprus from the British yoke sacrificing for this even my life.

'(2) I shall perform without objection all the instructions of the organization which may be entrusted to me and I shall not bring any objection, however difficult and dangerous these may be.

'(3) I shall not abandon the struggle unless I receive instructions from the leader of the organization and after our aim has been accomplished.

'(4) I shall never reveal to anyone any secret of our organization neither the names of my chiefs nor those of the other members of the organization even if I am caught and tortured.

'(5) I shall not reveal any of the instructions which may be given me even to my fellow combatants.

'If I disobey my oath, I shall be worthy of every punishment as a traitor and may eternal contempt cover me.

'E.O.K.A.'

The children among whom this pernicious organization was being set up were well prepared to receive it. Already in December 1954, when the United Nations refused to discuss the Cyprus problem, it was the children who had broken school discipline and staged demonstrations in the streets. In Nicosia and Limassol they rioted and clashed with the police; in the latter town they began stoning British troops who were standing by in support of the police, and the older boys became so violent that, after due warning, the troops were ordered to fire three separate shots, at intervals, into the crowd. Three youths were wounded and were at once hailed in Greece as well as in Cyprus as heroes and martyrs.

At this time Grivas personally had not much hold upon the children, but he soon strengthened it, and the next major demonstration, which was to be in Paphos when the trial came on of the men caught smuggling arms in the *St. George*, was ordered by Makarios, and stage-managed on Grivas's own instructions. He ordered that they were to prepare for demonstrations with mass singing and slogan-shouting. By February 1955 he was working the youth movement into the framework of E.O.K.A. itself and receiving personally the reports from its leader.

But before the next big demonstrations by school-children were to take place, the E.O.K.A. campaign of violence was itself to begin. By 21 March, Grivas was ready for the outbreak of violence. He had sabotage groups waiting in Nicosia, Larnaca, Famagusta and Limassol, each under its leader. These groups had already recon-noitred the selected targets, which were the radio stations at Athalassa and Lakatamia near Nicosia, barracks, Government offices, police stations and military instal-lations. He had distributed to the various groups a sufficient quantity of explosives, petrol and fuses, together with hand-grenades and some small bombs fitted with time-pencils. Now Grivas himself was waiting nervously in one of his hideouts in Nicosia for permis-sion from the Archbishop to begin the campaign; his only sortie was a quick trip to the mountains to meet the group leaders there.

On 29 March the Archbishop sent for Grivas and gave him the necessary permission to start. He also gave him his blessing. 'God is with us', noted Grivas. He decided to make the first operation on the night of 31 March/ 1 April. So he called together the four leaders who would conduct the affairs at Nicosia, Larnaca, Famagusta and Limassol for a final briefing. One of the subjects dis-cussed was where Grivas himself should go. They wanted him to hide in the little seaside holiday resort of Kyrenia, but he decided to stay near Nicosia, and early in the afternoon of 31 March, when the British would certainly all be at lunch, he moved to a house at Strovolos, close to Government House and the Secretariat. There he awaited the actions he had ordered, which were to take place at half an hour after midnight. The explosions in and around Nicosia he would himself be able to hear, but the first sign he expected that the work had started was to be the dowsing of the electric light, since part of the plan was to cut off the main electricity supply. At the appointed time there was a flicker in the light, but it came on again and Grivas feared failure; in fact, one youngster in the team that was to cut the cable had electrocuted himself. A few minutes later Grivas heard the first of the expected explosions, followed by others, and the biggest one last. There was nothing more he could do that night. He went to bed.

This first sabotage by E.O.K.A., the opening blow of the campaign of terrorism, was largely successful and took the authorities quite by surprise; where it failed, it did so only because of the incompetence of the saboteurs, not because of any alertness on the part of the police or the troops. The most successful piece of sabotage, for which Drakos was largely responsible, was at the Athalassa radio station near Nicosia, where the transmitter was destroyed. Military and government buildings were considerably damaged at Larnaca, where Poskotis and the other former P.E.O.N. leaders who had carried out the sabotage were arrested, and to a lesser degree at Limassol, where the commander got cold feet at the last moment, sat shivering in the car while his men tried to carry out the explosions, and then lost his head and succeeded in getting another leader arrested. When Grivas discovered this, he expelled the man from the organization, then spent days wondering whether he would turn traitor if the police picked him up. At Famagusta the operations were not very successful, and Afxentiou himself was detected, put on the wanted list by the police, and forced to go to ground in Lysi, his home town; for some days Grivas had no idea where he was.

Nevertheless, the campaign had begun with explosions that had caused damage estimated at £60,000. That same day, as further sporadic explosions took place all over the island, including one outside a Nicosia hotel which the Governor, Sir Robert Armitage, had just left, the first E.O.K.A. leaflets appeared signed by 'Dighenis', the Leader. This name, which Grivas had assumed, is that of a medieval Greek hero who is renowned in a long epic poem for defending territory on the outskirts of the empire.

Grivas could justifiably congratulate himself on having managed to pull off a surprise after he had been on the island for more than four months, during which time he had built up a workable military, sabotage and propaganda organization and put it into operation, although for most of the period his illegal presence in Cyprus had been suspected by the police.

There was, however, one source of irritation. From Athens Radio, the 'Voice of the Fatherland' programme directed to Cyprus had not only deprecated violence and mentioned the methods of Gandhi, but had let Savvas Loizides deliver a eulogy of his young brother, Sokratis. This was a bitter pill indeed, and Grivas wrote to the Archbishop a strong complaint.

CHAPTER IX

ONCE THE first blow had been struck and the first leaflet signed 'Dighenis' had been circulated, Grivas could bring into operation the second stage of his plan— to break the morale of the police force by attacks on police stations and on individual policemen, and to stimulate and frighten the general public into acquiescence with terrorism by the murder of a number of Greek sympathizers or collaborators with the British, and of the so-called 'traitors' to E.O.K.A. The original acts of sabotage of Government property and of rioting by schoolchildren would be continued, and indeed intensified, as the young men and women arrived at the state in which they were willing to throw bombs. And throughout, the propaganda campaign would be waged from Athens internationally, and within Cyprus by leaflet and slogan.

It is clear that for none of these purposes did Grivas himself require to be close to the scene of action. Indeed, it would be far better for him to retire to the most obscure hiding-place he could find, provided that he could manage to keep in touch with the assassins and saboteurs, the bomb-throwers and the pamphlet-distributors, and, of course, with the Archbishop and, through him, with the Athenian sponsors of the campaign. So long as several chains of messengers and couriers could be kept unbroken, the ideal place for

Grivas to establish himself and his small central command post was in the Troodos Mountains. He had already prepared there his hiding-places and organized his surrounding guard of mountain gangs and his elaborate messenger system, and soon after the first sabotage attack of 1 April 1955—though not immediately after—he went to the mountains. He established himself on the western slopes of the range, in close contact with the Kykko Monastery, around which he built his organization. A little later Afxentiou was similarly established on the eastern slopes, some twenty miles away, in contact with the Makheras Monastery. Afxentiou was always subsidiary to Grivas, and always carried out his orders with a military obedience that Grivas admired almost more than his determination. Around these two were scattered a few other mountain gangs of from six to ten men each, which offered reasonably secure havens to any assassins from the towns who needed to go into cover. For most of the time, and especially at first, these men led an agreeable enough life in the mountains. There were few troops about, and there was very little risk from the police. When in the evenings they went into the villages they were assured of plenty to eat and drink, and their romantic status as freedom fighters easily overcame the somewhat strict principles which normally rule the conduct of the young girls of Cyprus.

Grivas had not gone to the mountains to fight; there was, in fact, remarkably little actual fighting throughout the whole of the four years of E.O.K.A. He had gone there to hide and to direct terrorism throughout the island from a secure base. During those periods of 1955 that he 'spent in the mountains he was able to live in

considerable freedom, sleeping in village houses, or sometimes in Kykko Monastery itself, where one of his
blankets was later found. He knew, however, that this
could not last. He had therefore prepared, in several
places in that area, a number of underground hides.
They were not usually caves—caves were such obvious
places to search—but underground passages and small
rooms hewn out from the mountainside. The entrances
to these hides were very narrow and small, and always
elaborately camouflaged. Sometimes they were beneath
overhanging vegetation on the side of a bank. More often
they were small holes in the ground, usually in stony
places—because excavated earth shows a different colour
when it is replaced, but replaced stones cannot easily be
detected. Whenever possible, these entrances were sited
among plantations of young trees or saplings, and, of
course, far from any footpaths. Great care was taken to
make the cover to the entrance absolutely solid, so that
a man could walk over it without feeling any difference.
Grivas claims that, in fact, British troops on several later
occasions walked over mountain hides in which he was
sitting in silence, and had no idea that he was just beneath their feet.

His ability to stay still for days and sometimes for
weeks on end, in some small underground room hollowed from a mountainside, while troops searching for
him were passing by or over the concealed entrance, was
Grivas's most powerful personal weapon. The feat called
for unfaltering nerve and for disregard of acute physical
discomfort. The worst experience he had of this kind was
in an underground hide near the village of Milikouri,
just south of the Kykko Monastery in the Troodos
Mountains. Grivas went to earth in this hide when

considerable forces of British troops moved into the area and began an intensive search for him, which pinned him down for some five weeks. The troops never discovered the small entrance to the hide, which was extremely well hidden under solid rocks, but they got so close to it that for several days Grivas had to remain in the hide alone, and none of his own men could get near him. He had to sit all the time alone, in silence, in a cramped space, sometimes dozing, sometimes waking, and never knowing how long it would be before the troops moved off and enabled his lieutenants to open up his hide and get him out. He had enough food and water to last out a considerable siege. But what he had not reckoned on was a mole which was burrowing actively in the earth close to his underground room. The mole's tunnelling opened up connexion with the bed of a small stream, and water began to filter into Grivas's hiding-place. He watched it with apprehension, not knowing how high it would rise, or whether it would fill the cavern and force him out. In fact, it rose no higher than his ankles. But for the remaining days he was forced to sit with his feet in water.

In time these hides became more and more elaborate. There was one, for example, in the 'panhandle'—the peninsula of eastern Cyprus—which was entered from the bottom of the shaft of a village well, just above the water-level. It consisted of two underground passages each big enough for two men to walk abreast in comfort. One, about 60 yards long and ventilated by the shaft of another disused well, led to an emergency exit (or entrance) beneath overhanging foliage on a bank further down the valley; the entrance itself was only just big enough for a slim man to wriggle through. The other passage was shorter and led to an underground room hewn out of rock. The obvious intention was to continue this passage towards a nearby house, where it would terminate under some hidden trap-door or in the space inside a wall.

By no means all of the hides were in the open. Many were constructed inside houses, churches and monasteries, just as the priest-holes were made in the manor houses of England during the persecution of the Catholics. They were usually small cellars hollowed out beneath the floor of one of the main rooms. The top of the cellar was roofed in with thick slabs of stone so that there would be no indication to anybody walking above that there was a hollow beneath and so that a probing bayonet could not find a cavity.

The entrances to these domestic hides were variously placed. A favourite was the stone slab beneath the fire in the hearth which could be swung up to allow access to a secret passage below. In the early days some of these hides were constructed with insufficient consideration of practical difficulties. One cold night, for example, a British patrol entered a village house in the course of a normal search operation. All seemed quiet—a peaceful domestic scene of a family sitting around the hearth. The British officer noticed, however, that the fire had only just been lit. He brushed the burning sticks to one side, pressed on the stone slab, and it opened to reveal a passage below, from which two terrorists came running up into capture with evident relief. The officer discovered why when he went down to inspect the underground hide. He took a candle with him and as he descended the stairs it guttered out. The fire on the hearth above had drawn off most of the oxygen and had they been forced to remain there for many more minutes the terrorists would have died of suffocation.

As they grew more experienced, however, the E.O.K.A. men soon avoided mistakes of that sort. They constructed series of hides, in the open and in houses, which led by easy stages from one position of advantage to another. There was, for instance, a chain of hides that led from the vicinity of the Kykko Monastery right down into Limassol on the southern coast of the island, beyond the Troodos foothills. This was frequently used by Grivas himself. The chain led across the southern slope of the mountains into the foothills nearest to Limassol, around the village of Mathikoloni, and thus down into various houses in Limassol. One of the house hides was discovered eventually by some British troops, almost by accident. It was beneath the tiled floor of a bathroom. The four tiles beneath the hand-basin, each about 9 inches square, were joined together to make a trap-door. But this trap was so balanced that it would open only if a foot was pressed down on the tiles right up against the bathroom wall—an unlikely place to be trodden on by accident, since the hand-basin was above. Beneath the trap-door was a hollowed-out hide just big enough for a man to stand up in; he could not have sat down.

The discovery of this hide caused a few red faces. The bathroom had been for some time that of a British Intelligence officer.

During the course of operations, British troops, mostly Royal Engineers, discovered scores of these hides and blew them up. Towards the end, the Sappers got a new piece of secret electronic equipment which would reveal whether a floor or a wall were solid or whether there was a space behind and how big that space was.

Once this equipment was put into operation the detection of hides was greatly accelerated. Had it been available from the start it is doubtful whether Grivas himself could have avoided capture. But it came too late. By the end of the operations, it is certain that there were still hundreds of these hides undiscovered. They were half the reason that Grivas remained free.

The other half was his system of communications, his network of messengers.

In the mountains these were all men, though some of them for camouflage purposes were given female code-names; in the towns quite a lot of the messengers were girls. For several reasons the system of communication was slow. One was that not only were the messengers unaware of Grivas's hiding-place, but they were usually unknown to each other.

Another reason was that many of the messages they carried were not written down, but learned by heart. If Grivas, in the mountains, wished to send an important message, he wrote it himself and one of the two or three men who knew where he was then took it to a nearby place, to which a messenger was summoned. The messenger was told to learn it by heart, and was made to recite it over and over again until he was word-perfect. Since many of these messengers were uneducated village lads, this task often took two days. When he went off to deliver the message—to recite it, that is, to somebody in Nicosia who could take it down—he carried an E.O.K.A. leaflet in his pocket. The penalty for possessing one was three years' imprisonment. If the messenger was followed by the police and thought he was in danger of arrest, he was instructed to hand out the leaflet rather obviously, so that he would be arrested for that, and nobody would think of enquiring further into his activities. He would simply be locked up. He was then of no further use to E.O.K.A.; but he had also been of no use to the British.

It is clear that such methods were bound to lead to considerable delays; there were times when the E.O.K.A. headquarters in Nicosia was out of touch with Grivas for as long as three weeks, even though two or three messengers had been sent by different routes to convey the same message. Not all the messages, of course, were sent verbally. Many were written down and carried at greater risk, but with much more speed. There were several reception centres for messages in all the larger towns. The chief one close to Nicosia was in the Kykko Monastery annexe; others were in shops in the old town of Nicosia, where the shopkeepers acted, sometimes under duress, as E.O.K.A. post-boxes.

The terrorist campaign which Grivas conducted after his first sabotage blow on 1 April 1955 went very slowly. His success continued among the schoolchildren, who duly rioted in Paphos when the gun-runners came up for trial (Sokratis Loizides got twelve years, and was headed for Wormwood Scrubs and Maidstone gaols). When the sentences were announced, pupils went on strike in protest and in Nicosia and Famagusta streamed into the streets and stoned the police. The Nicosia riots were limited by the Headmaster of the Pancyprian Gymnasium, who, together with some of the teachers, ran after the pupils and persuaded them back into their classrooms. This 'treachery' infuriated Grivas, who wrote a bitter complaint to the Archbishop. Later the Headmaster was beaten up by his pupils in his own home and subsequently acquiesced in whatever E.O.K.A. ordered the children to do. By the autumn the senior schoolboys were ready to throw bombs, and some of them to carry out assassinations with revolvers. The plan of corruption, from shouting slogans to committing murder, involving the boy ever more deeply at every step, was working well.

But the general campaign of terrorism, and especially the first assault which Grivas had ordered against the police, was at best lackadaisical. After a little haphazard bomb-throwing in April and an unsuccessful attempt to dynamite a village police station near Nicosia, activity died down until the latter part of June, when Grivas had ordered a series of co-ordinated attacks on police stations. Masked men attempted to carry out these attacks, sometimes by gunfire, more often by exploding bombs, but little damage was done and only one policeman was injured; the most serious was the explosion of a bomb which had been slipped into the letter-box of Nicosia's central police station and which killed one passing Greek civilian and injured thirteen Turks and Armenians. Grivas was disappointed at the lack of enterprise shown by his terrorists and noted: 'Our men in the towns have lost their courage.' In spite of harshly threatening statements from the Archbishop, and sermons by the Bishop of Kyrenia calling from the pulpit for the sacrifice of blood, it seemed difficult to persuade the young men to kill anybody. Occasional bombs were tossed through the open doors of bars, or the windows of private houses where British military families lived, but many of them failed to explode, and those that did caused no casualties. Athens Radio screamed of bloodshed and oppression, but there was little of either. In fact, Grivas was glad of an excuse to order a temporary suspension on political grounds of the activities which he could not intimidate his gunmen into carrying out. The excuse was that the British Government, in an endeavour to stop the dreadful business before it got really serious, called a Tripartite Conference in London to which the Greek and Turkish Governments were invited.

The Athens propagandists claimed that this conference was the result of the impression made on public opinion by the outburst of violence in Cyprus. And they were right. Grivas's plan was already working as he intended that it should. By August he was ready to renew the terrorism, and at last it began to be effective. On 10 August a Greek Cypriot special constable was shot dead in the streets of Nicosia and a police sergeant outside a club in Famagusta. At the end of the month a Greek Cypriot police constable named Poullis was shot dead in a crowded street in Nicosia while he was on duty at a Communist mass meeting. This time the lad who shot him, a youngster named Michael Karaolis, was caught and charged with murder. He was arrested just as he was being driven away to join an E.O.K.A. gang in the Kyrenia Mountains. When he came to trial a couple of months later he was convicted, and was the first E.O.K.A. gunman to be sentenced to death.

Meanwhile, the Tripartite Conference in London had failed, as it was bound to do, and on 25 September, Field-Marshal Sir John Harding, formerly Chief of the Imperial General Staff, was appointed Governor of Cyprus. He was sworn in on 3 October. He took personal command of the anti-terrorist operations, strongly reinforced his military strength, and brought out from Britain 300 policemen of all ranks to stiffen the Cyprus police, restore their morale, and try to weed out from among them those members who were secret members of E.O.K.A.; in this last task they never succeeded.

The state of the island as Sir John Harding found it was deplorable. For all its amateur quality, E.O.K.A. had been able to operate much as it liked. On occasions E.O.K.A. men had travelled from one town to another in British Army lorries, sometimes with a false police escort and sometimes without. The E.O.K.A. members had also delighted in playing off against each other the rival forces which were attempting to catch Grivas—the Army and the Cyprus police. Sometimes they were given simultaneous, but different tips as to where Grivas would be at a certain time; both were false. If a piece of true information were given, it was to the police—but it was given late. They were told at one time, for example, that he would be in a small village outside Paphos. This was true, but the timing was wrong. A co-ordinated intelligence force would probably have caught him, but E.O.K.A. knew that the Cyprus police were so intent on claiming the honour of trapping him that they would keep the information to themselves, set out in inadequate numbers, and so miss him. The object of that operation from E.O.K.A. point of view was, of course, to give the police confidence in a particular informer, who could afterwards be used to pass false information.

When Sir John first arrived the morale of the police was so low, the security forces were in so precarious a state, and the combination of threat and patriotic propaganda had placed Greek-Cypriot public opinion so firmly on Grivas's side that the new Governor thought it possible that E.O.K.A. might bring about a general uprising of the population. But Grivas never really intended this. What he wanted was a state of constant chaos and crisis which would eventually influence world opinion so strongly that Britain would be forced to surrender the island to Greece.

The actions taken by Sir John Harding in stiffening and strengthening the security forces, inevitable as they may have been in conditions of growing lawlessness, were precisely those that best suited Grivas's purposes. They produced just those circumstances in which the Cypriot population would be inflamed against the British and in which the E.O.K.A. campaign of sabotage and murder could more easily be presented as a heroic national struggle for freedom from an oppressor.

When Sir John first arrived, and went the next day to open talks with Archbishop Makarios, there seemed considerable hope that the state of terrorism might be checked and the crisis averted. The talks at first went well. But as they progressed, Grivas, acting on instructions, simultaneously moved the E.O.K.A. campaign into its third stage—the attack on the British themselves. Towards the end of October the first British soldier to be killed in the emergency, Lance-Corporal A. R. L. Milne, died when a bomb was thrown at a military vehicle in Kissonerga. By the end of the following month Grivas had his assassins thoroughly in hand. An attempt was made by Markos Drakos on the Governor's own life by a bomb explosion in the Ledra Palace Hotel in Nicosia; in fact, he was not there. Five British soldiers were killed within a week, two of them ambushed, one in a bomb explosion in a sergeant's mess in Nicosia, one shot in the chest in Dhekelia, and—most ominous signal —the fifth shot in the back as he walked down a Nicosia street. The assassination pattern had been set. Whenever there was a street killing, the body lay there on the roadway and nobody in all the crowd had seen or heard anything. For terror had now gained its way. The bombs and the bullets had provided the final argument for holding the tongue.

The Governor declared a state of emergency.

CHAPTER X

As the talks between the new Governor and the Archbishop straggled spasmodically on throughout December 1955 and the following January and February, Grivas, from his hideout in the Troodos Mountains, ordered that the attacks on British troops and civilians, and on Greek Cypriots whom he regarded as traitors or collaborators with the British, should be intensified. The British Government, still trying to pacify, announced a development plan for Cyprus that would cost £38 million. There was some momentary hope when, after the death of Field-Marshal Papagos, Mr. Karamanlis became the new Prime Minister of Greece; but he was unable to take any attitude other than to continue to support the rebels in Cyprus. At the end of February, when it seemed that there might after all be a successful conclusion to the talks with the Archbishop, the Colonial Secretary, Mr. Lennox Boyd, flew out to Cyprus to join in with his authority.

But all this went on against a background of continued general rioting and an increasing number of assassinations ordered by Grivas, and no doubt consented to by the Archbishop.

The schoolchildren, when they got back from their summer holidays, during which they had been indoctrinated in their villages, had been worked up into a far more militant mood. E.O.K.A. cells in the classrooms now had control, and all other discipline, by teachers or parents, had broken down. In January, Grivas circulated to the children two leaflets urging them to violence, couched in his usual florid style: 'You have been suckled by the running waters of heroic acts and now you spring up active from a holocaust.' One leaflet urged the children of the Greeks to 'liberate the Fatherland', and 'strike the tyrant'. And in words that might have been borrowed from an earlier German dictatorship, Grivas continued: 'Cyprus commands, and not the school. Cyprus commands, and not the family. The Fatherland is more honest, more decent, and more sacred than the father, the mother and all other ancestors. Cyprus commands, and her command is sacred. School and family give way to it. . . .'

It was on incitement of this kind that the children rioted through the streets, stoning the police and security forces, pushing the schoolgirls to the front to embarrass the troops, on such occasions as the failure of Michael Karaolis's appeal against his death sentence for the murder of P.C. Poullis. As a result of these riots, some of the schools had to be closed. It was on such incitement that gangs of youths raided by night, and broke up, the elementary schools, in which Grivas was not having the same success; and went round threatening shopkeepers who failed to obey Grivas's order to put up the shutters; or tossed a bomb which killed a Marine sergeant; or burned down a post office. It was a schoolboy who tossed a bomb through the open window of a house in Larnaca where Mrs. Smith, wife of a British Army sergeant, flung herself across her two young children whom she was putting to bed, saving them from injury, but herself losing her right foot. And it was the responsibility of Grivas, who put explosives into the hands of children, that so many of them killed themselves or their younger brothers and sisters with weapons they did not understand, or had abandoned in fright by the roadside. A typical story is that of four children, all under nine years of age, who found a bomb in an orange grove at Lapithos which exploded as they played with it, killing one of them and maiming the three others for life.

In the towns and villages the campaign of violence was sporadic, and usually not pressed home. Most of the bombs thrown wildly at police stations did little damage. Most of the explosions that occurred in Nicosia on special occasions, as, for instance, just when Mr. Lennox Boyd was about to meet the Archbishop, caused no casualties. But the few young men whom Grivas had brought to the point of assassination were growing bolder. Their worst crime was in February, when two of them, heavily masked and wearing black robes, entered the Chrysoroyiatissa Monastery. While one of them covered the monks with a revolver, the other killed the Abbot, who was wrongly suspected of having betrayed two arrested terrorists, with a double-barrelled shotgun.

The most dastardly attempt, specifically ordered by Grivas, which fortunately failed, was placing a time-bomb in a transport aircraft at Nicosia Airport, with the fuse set to explode soon after it had taken off from Singapore with forty-four Service families on board; by chance, the take-off was delayed, and the aircraft was wrecked on the ground, with nobody in it. After this, R.A.F. security was thoroughly overhauled.

It was not until this time that it became generally known that Dighenis, the E.O.K.A. leader, was in fact

George Grivas, of whose illegal entry into the island the police had been aware for more than a year.

The talks between the Colonial Secretary, the Governor and the Archbishop failed at the end of February 1956. The British had agreed to self-determination for Cyprus at an unspecified date, and proposed to send a Constitutional Commissioner to the island that summer to draw up a Constitution. It was not upon these main considerations that the talks broke down, but upon quite minor points. Mr. Lennox Boyd therefore returned to England, and Sir John Harding prepared to restore law and order by force. His next step, on 9 March, was to deport Archbishop Makarios, the Bishop of Kyrenia, and two others. The Archbishop was about to fly to Athens. At Nicosia Airport he was diverted to an R.A.F. aircraft, to which the other deportees had also been brought. They were flown to Kenya, and then to exile at Mahe in the Seychelles Islands. That day, the Governor issued a long statement setting forth the evidence that the Archbishop was personally deeply implicated in the campaign of terrorism by E.O.K.A.

Whether these actions were wisely taken or not—and Grivas claims that Sir John Harding played into his hands by providing better propaganda material than Grivas himself had ever hoped for—they radically altered the situation in Cyprus itself. Grivas and E.O.K.A. had for some time commanded the allegiance of most of the villagers and of the poorer Greeks in the Cypriot towns, because they had been indoctrinated by their priests, they feared the terrorism, and were people of strong family ties who automatically came to the aid of their children, over whom Grivas had almost complete control. But many of the better-educated Cypriot Greeks had been by no means convinced. Now, as the Harding measures tightened, they found themselves falling into emotional agreement with E.O.K.A., in spite of the murders and the outrages committed by the gunmen and the bomb-throwers, which they genuinely came to accept as justifiable in the struggle for freedom. As one of the leading lawyers of the island put it: 'To the world outside the Greeks, these young men may have seemed murderers. To the Greeks, and to us in Cyprus, they were heroes fighting for our liberation. It may not have been rational, but that is how we all came to feel. It was emotional.' Some of the measures which swung these people behind Grivas were quite trivial—indignities rather than sufferings. They resented mass searches in which they were ordered out of their cars, perhaps in the presence of their wives, and made to stand facing a wall, hands up, while troops searched their clothing. They were bitter about punitive measures which followed the killings, as when, if no witness would come forward, the surrounding buildings were cleared of their inhabitants, sealed and left empty for several months. The Cypriots argued that quite often they in fact had no evidence to give; they had merely caught sight of a youth, whom they did not know, in a white shirt, bolting round a corner after the gunshot. But even if they had evidence, they said frankly that they would not dream of giving it, because if they did they would themselves be shot within twenty-four hours.

In this frame of mind, the Cypriots were also far more receptive to propaganda of the most vicious kind which was by now pouring into Cyprus from Athens Radio (which, soon after, had to be jammed). Intelligent Cypriots were able to believe, and they still believe, that

British troops and police were behaving with the most astonishing brutality towards people they rounded up for interrogation, and towards the general population. These allegations ranged from declaring that the British were flogging, forcing men to stand on nails or on ice, and injecting them with narcotics, to tearing out fingernails, rape and the beating-up of pregnant women. In fact, there were six cases brought against policemen, and one case against two Army officers. In three of the cases the policemen were acquitted by the court; in two there were convictions for minor assaults which consisted of using more force than was necessary to effect an arrest, and in one a constable was sentenced to three years' imprisonment for firing a gun and wounding two Cypriots. The two Army officers were court-martialled and convicted of beating a prisoner, and were dismissed from the Service.

Aside from these specific cases, the truth of the general allegations of British brutality and torture can be assessed from the happenings at a village called Milikouri in the Troodos Mountains, which was kept under curfew for fifty-four days during a military operation against mountain E.O.K.A. gangs. Allegations were published that the villagers were being submitted to the most fearful tortures, and that they and their animals were being left to die of disease and starvation. When the curfew ended, Press correspondents were taken to Milikouri, where the villagers cheerfully reported that they were all very well, nobody had been assaulted, two British doctors had been in attendance throughout the period, food and mail had been brought in from outside, and the Government itself had provided a lot of free food (to the value, in fact, of about £1,000).

None of these refutations, however, served to diminish the solidarity with which the Greek population of Cyprus ranged itself behind Grivas and E.O.K.A. Genuine emotion now reinforced fear of reprisals, and the security forces of troops and police were compelled to work in the midst of a hostile civil population.

One of the methods used was that of mass arrests and interrogation following a murder. Grivas regarded this with special approval, not simply because it was helping to weld the Greek population to his side, but because it was clumsy police work. The police arrested too many people. When they had got them into detention camps, there were insufficient Greek-speaking police who could be trusted to carry out the interrogations. Some of the people whom they arrested, and held for a short time in camps, were in fact men who were close to Grivas, and who did not know that they were under suspicion. Had they been left alone and followed, instead of being arrested and detained, there were at least two of them who would have led the police to Grivas in 1955 and the early months of 1956. One of these was Markos Drakos, who was arrested in the summer of 1955 and held in the old castle at Kyrenia, from which, in the autumn, he escaped to join Grivas in the mountains.

When the Scotland Yard men who were brought in had properly assessed the situation, they realized that too many arrests were being made. But by then it was too late. Grivas had seen the danger too, and had tightened his security so effectively that almost nobody in the island knew where he was at any one time, and the courier system had become so intricate that it was unlikely that any single chain could be followed right to the end.

Violence in the towns and villages increased after the deportation of Makarios. Schoolboys on bicycles went racing round the shopping streets, warning all shop-keepers to close for two days, on Grivas's orders, on pain of death. Assassins murdered policemen and troops in the streets, usually shooting them in the back and then bolting. There were casualties from bomb-throwing, casualties from fire. Priests stood on the pavements urging on mobs of rioting schoolchildren, who some-times grew so violent that they had to be dispersed with tear-gas. Another attempt was made on the life of Sir John Harding, and this one nearly succeeded. A young domestic servant in Government House placed a bomb beneath the mattress of his bed, and the Governor slept on it for one night. The time-fuse was not in proper working order. Next day the servant was seen bicycling hastily into Nicosia, and, suspicious, the security forces carried out a search and found the bomb, which was removed to a rubbish dump outside by a young British officer; it exploded five minutes later.

There were two significant developments in the plan of violence, one premeditated, the other not.

Grivas decided to take his plan one stage further by ordering the murder of British civilians. He contrived that the first should be assassinated on 1 April 1956—the first anniversary of the outbreak of terrorism in Cyprus. The civilian, Mr. J. C. Cooke, who was attached to Army headquarters at Episkopi, was shot in the back with a 0.38 revolver in Gladstone Street, Limassol. The shot also wounded a young Cypriot woman who hap-pened to be passing nearby.

The second development began with the first deliber-ate murder of a Turkish Cypriot. He was a police sergeant named Abdullah Ali Riza, who lived at Paphos. As he came out of his house, four E.O.K.A. men opened fire on him. He managed to draw his revolver and return the fire, but he missed his assailants, and was himself already dying of his wounds. At once, Turks began attacking Greek shops in Nicosia. They were dispersed by the leader of the Turkish Cypriots, Dr. Fazil Kutchuk.

The next incident happened in Nicosia during April, when two E.O.K.A. gunmen fired at a police constable and were seen and chased by an unarmed Turkish Cypriot policeman who was off duty, but happened to be passing. The gunmen lost their heads and, as this policeman, who was named Nihad, overtook them, turned and shot him dead. The two youths jumped on bicycles to get away, but a seventeen-year-old Turkish girl grabbed hold of one of them, pulled him off balance, and succeeded in holding him until help arrived. All this was followed by renewed rioting by Turks against Greeks.

A month later it happened again, this time deliberately. E.O.K.A. gunmen went into a coffee-shop at Polis and shot a Turkish police constable named Lisani Ahmed who was sitting there. This time the Turkish crowd almost got out of hand. All Turkish shops were shut, a Greek priest stoned, fighting with knives and clubs broke out between groups of either community, buildings on both sides were set on fire, a Greek watchman at a factory was beaten to death, and a curfew had to be imposed on the Turkish quarters of Nicosia.

The most brutal of the E.O.K.A. murders committed at this time was that of an Assistant Superintendent of Police named Aristotelous, who had been to London for a course of training. Grivas had specifically ordered this man's death before he went, but the job was bungled.

On his return, Aristotelous went to a Nicosia clinic to visit his wife, who had just given birth to their first child. Two E.O.K.A. men entered the clinic and shot him, escaping afterwards in a stolen car. Grivas then put out a pamphlet boasting that he had given instructions for this assassination.

Executions also continued of Greeks whom Grivas had condemned as 'traitors'. One of these, though E.O.K.A. tried weakly to deny responsibility, was a man named Manolis Pierides, who was shot dead in his stall at Kythrea Church by four masked men who entered during a service.

There undoubtedly were collaborators with the British security forces; the more successfully the British waged the struggle against Grivas, the more informers came forward; on the other hand, if Grivas seemed to be getting the upper hand once again, the supply of information to the security forces dried up. Some of these informers agreed to be taken to a village and, from a hidden position, to point out men who were to their knowledge E.O.K.A. members. How accurate this information was, was often highly doubtful. And on some occasions the British cloaking of the informers was clumsily handled, their identity was revealed, and they were afterwards shot.

Not that it was always necessary for the British to have slipped up in order for the informer's identity to be known. In Cyprus, where everybody knows everybody, and gossip is the perpetual occupation, suspicions were very easily aroused. Grivas had a system which he frequently put into operation against a suspect. An E.O.K.A man gave the suspect a piece of false information. If he was a traitor, it would be passed on to the police within forty-eight hours. The fact that it was passed on was known to Grivas, because E.O.K.A. had made considerable penetrations into the police. Grivas himself passed the final verdict on all persons accused of treachery, and instructions for their execution went in his name, by messenger, and via the various E.O.K.A. postboxes, to the leader of the killer group, in the appropriate district.

CHAPTER XI

A T HIS command post in the mountains, where he had not as yet been seriously troubled, Grivas knew that his personal security would soon be challenged. There was now a price of £10,000 on his head (plus a free passage to anywhere in the world for anyone giving information that would lead to his arrest), and his lieutenants on the 'Wanted' list bore prices of £5,000.

For all his low opinion of Sir John Harding's political tactics, Grivas never for a moment underestimated him as a soldier. 'He is a field-marshal', he remarked to one of his headquarters men, 'and a clever soldier.' Grivas knew that Sir John was setting up for the first time an efficient and co-ordinated Intelligence machine, and that he could scarcely much longer be in doubt as to where Grivas was hiding, if only in general terms. He therefore expected the all-out assault on his Troodos Mountain positions which Sir John was in fact preparing.

Throughout the winter of 1955-6, troops stationed in the western half of Cyprus had been probing into the mountains, searching villages, setting up road-blocks, carrying out patrols, and they had already seized several of Grivas's stragglers and discovered some of their hide-out caves, stocked with arms and ammunition, food and clothing. At that time of the year, of course, the mountains were snow-covered, and operations had to be carried out in intense cold. In retaliation for the probing,

Grivas set his mountain gangs to lay ambushes for British military vehicles. The ambushes were carried out with rifles and automatic weapons, and led to virtually the only real guerrilla fighting that E.O.K.A. ever undertook. The most successful of these encounters from Grivas's point of view was when the first of a convoy of vehicles of the Gordon Highlanders ran into an ambush. The following drivers, not yet accustomed to the drill, did not realize that there was trouble, and drew their vehicles close up behind. The British troops suffered several casualties before reinforcements arrived and it was possible to drive the guerrillas away.

While this particular action was encouraging to Grivas, he was well aware, as a soldier, that it was a flash in the pan, and that he would never, during the course of the campaign, be able to train his guerrillas to fight trained troops, to press home attacks, or indeed to withstand assaults that they could easily have driven off. The most outstanding example of that was the ambush in which Major Brian Coombes was trapped. On 15 December 1955 he was returning from a reconnaissance and was on what was thought to be a safe road near Lefka, north of the Troodos Mountains range. Major Coombes himself happened at that time to be driving, and his driver was in the seat beside him. As they rounded a bend in the road, a shot was fired that smashed the windscreen and killed his driver. Coombes then pulled the vehicle into the side of the road, under shelter from an overhanging rock, seized his Sten gun and rushed up the hillside, to find to his surprise that the ambushers—there were four of them—were still in the gully from which they had fired, and he had got behind them. He opened fire and wounded one; the three others ducked for cover.

Of these four E.O.K.A. men, two were among Grivas's favourite lieutenants—Markos Drakos, the former clerk and P.E.O.N. organizer who became the first E.O.K.A. district commander in Nicosia, and escaped from imprisonment in Kyrenia Castle—and Haralambos Mouskos, a cousin of Archbishop Makarios, who had already taken part in several ambushes, had been wounded, and had lain up in the Kykko Monastery to receive treatment for his wounds.

After the first few exchanges of fire, Major Coombes realized that he had run out of ammunition. He therefore slipped back to the road, took his driver's loaded gun, stopped a lorry travelling on the road and gave the driver a message to take to the nearest Army post, and worked his way back up the hill to find that the terrorists were still there. He called to them to surrender, and after a time they said they would. One of them stood up, but as Coombes came forward to get him, Mouskos tried to shoot him from a hidden position. Coombes, however, got his burst in first, and killed Mouskos. The fourth man, who was Drakos, made a dash for the crest of the hill. Coombes, who had no more ammunition in the Sten gun, tried to get him with a revolver, but missed, and Drakos got back to the mountains, where he at once reported to Grivas. Meanwhile, Coombes sat opposite the two remaining live terrorists, fervently hoping that they did not know he was out of ammunition, and waiting anxiously for the sound of approaching reinforcements, wondering whether they would be those of the Army or of E.O.K.A. They were of the Army.

While these preliminary brushes were taking place, Grivas was keying up his sources of intelligence to give him the longest possible warning of the major attack he knew to be impending. He had already seen, at the end of April, that the British troops were quietly setting up new observation posts. He therefore circulated an order to the leaders of all his mountain gangs, giving them his very accurate estimate of the situation—that the next few weeks would be critical for E.O.K.A. He forbade all movement of E.O.K.A. guerrillas during the hours of daylight. If any movement simply had to be made during daylight, then they were to move separately and at the lengthy intervals which Grivas had lain down in the rules he had inculcated into all of them. He himself moved rather further away to the south from his hide near Kykko Monastery.

In the early days of May, the British assault on E.O.K.A. in the mountains was launched. It was a combined operation by the Royal Navy, the Royal Marine Commandos, the Army, helicopters of the R.A.F., and the police with their tracker dogs.

The first operations were carried out by troops already stationed in the area, chiefly the Gordon Highlanders and the Marine Commandos. It was an informer who first put them on the track of some caves in the mountains above Polis, that had recently been used by one of Grivas's gang. They surprised five terrorists close by and captured them, and in the caves themselves discovered considerable quantities of ammunition and other supplies. The caves themselves had boarded sides, timbered floors and corrugated-iron ceilings. They were set deep into the mountainside, and well camouflaged.

The major operation opened on 17 May. The Navy patrolled the coast from Polis to Karovastasi, on the north-west of Cyprus, and the troops surrounded the countryside for about twenty miles inland. They moved

into the area by night and with no lights on their vehicles
—there was not a single accident, a remarkable achievement on those mountain roads. To produce the necessary
surprise, they got out of their vehicles many miles from
their selected positions, and force-marched to them
across the mountains in darkness; one party covered
twenty miles. At daybreak a patrol of the Parachute
Regiment almost bumped into the first mountain gang
to be contacted. Without attempting to put up a fight, the
E.O.K.A. men dropped most of their arms and fled, with
the Parachutists harrying them through the mountains.
It was on the British left flank—the northern sector of
the operations, around Lefka, Ambelikou and Kambos—
that the greatest successes were gained, and two gang
leaders with £5,000 on their heads were caught by 20
May. A large number of hides were uncovered; Grivas
got a report from one of his men that a traitor had been
taken up in a helicopter, and had pointed out their
situation to the British. As was usual, once some of the
terrorists had been caught, they started to talk; and once
it was seen in the villages that the gangs looked like being
broken up, more and more information was passed to the
troops. As a result very largely of this, some seventeen
of the guerrillas were captured in all, together with a lot
of explosives, arms and ammunition, and supplies rang-
ing from food and clothing and a Sam Browne belt, to a
tent found in one of the underground hides.

Throughout all this, Grivas himself was following
his set tactic of going to ground and staying still. He
expected his surrounding gangs to attempt to fight—they
noticeably did not—but he himself had no intention of
taking part in any gun-battles except in the direst
emergency. In this he was, from his own point of view,

perfectly correct. His objective was solely to stay free so that he could later resume control of the campaign of sporadic violence in the towns that could be turned to good propaganda account. He therefore lay still in a hide not far from Kykko Monastery—eight were discovered within three miles of it, and in one was a letter from a priest at the monastery—and waited. He was still in touch, through couriers who moved only by night, with some few of his gangs, and chiefly with Markos Drakos, the terrorist who had escaped from Major Coombes, and who was now the only important gang leader in close touch with Grivas.

On 21 May the British assault changed its pattern. There was by now sufficient Intelligence to narrow the area considerably and to concentrate on a much more careful search that thoroughly scoured the ground. And this flushed Grivas out.

With a few companions, he began to move. But his difficulty was that he was now encircled by the searching troops, who were closing in on the heights south of Kykko Monastery from Milikouri, Peravasa, and Panayia—little villages connected by dirt roads which were Grivas's biggest problem, since all were closely watched. On 25 and 26 May he was nearly caught. He was crouched behind some bushes within a few yards of a British patrol when he was seen. The British troops were uncertain for the moment, however, whether they might not be facing another patrol of their own side, and they hesitated to fire. The slight pause was sufficient to allow Grivas to turn and plunge into the thick forest.

Not long afterwards he had his closest escape of all. He was making his way through the forest with only one man close to him when they heard a British patrol coming, wriggled into a bush and lay still. One of the soldiers came to within a couple of yards of Grivas, and suddenly called out to the other, 'Here. Over here.'

Grivas was on the point of shooting. This was the last thing he wanted to do, since it would betray his position, and bring an immediate return of fire. He hesitated for a moment. The rest of the patrol came over. And then Grivas realized that when the first soldier had shouted, 'Over here,' he meant he had found a path for them to follow. The patrol moved away along the path without spotting the two men lying motionless beneath a bush.

There were tracker dogs in the vicinity, but their handlers, who had kept up a spanking pace for days over the most tiring mountain country, could no longer maintain it. Grivas himself was also nearly exhausted, and on the point of cracking. Fit though he was, his age was against him. He was cut off from all communication with his gangs, except for the few men who were with him. His mountain organization had been virtually destroyed, and his chief communications centre discovered in Kykko Monastery. He noted in his diary, on 25 May: 'This day is the worst of the struggle for me.' But he managed to get to another underground hide, high up on the peak that towers to the west above Milikouri, where he lay up for a couple of days, and where couriers managed to make contact with him again, and he learned where, at any rate, Drakos and his men were. But he could not stay there. British patrols were passing close to the entrance to his hide. They had not so far discovered it, but an even more intensive search might do so. Throughout the night of 27/28 May he worked his way most dangerously round precipitous mountain slopes to a hide that lay on the southern side of the main peak of the area. He called this, on account of the steepness of the ground that had to be crossed in darkness, the most dangerous march of his life. When he and his companions reached this hide, they were completely exhausted, and once more, for a time, cut off from all communication with anyone, though they knew where Drakos was.

The action against Grivas was by no means ended, however. Not only was more information coming in to the British Intelligence service, but the captured terrorists, and particularly the gang leaders who were closest to Grivas, had talked. It was therefore known that he was in an area of the thickly wooded Paphos forest that covers about 400 square miles to the west of Mount Troodos. On 7 June British headquarters were set up at Kykko Monastery, on the northern perimeter of the area, and a general cordon was put around it which aimed in particular at cutting routes from the mountains to the villages.

The first suspicion Grivas had of this—for once his Intelligence sources had failed him—was at half-past two on the morning of 8 June. He was woken by the barking of a dog, and, since he knew that no dog would ordinarily be that high up on the mountain at night, guessed that the security forces were nearer.

He woke the men with him, and soon afterwards they crawled from the hide and climbed to the crest of a ridge, from which they could watch the Milikouri road. As dawn broke, they saw four two-ton British Army lorries travelling the road. One of them stopped and dropped off two of Grivas's gang-leaders who, having been captured earlier, had betrayed him.

What Grivas now intended to do was to make use of

the chain of hides that led towards Limassol, where he could go to earth in a house. His problem was first to break out of the encircling troops, who were obviously now well informed of his likely movements. And the first part of the problem was to get across the dirt road from Paravasa to Panayia, which was closely watched. He sent some scouts forward. They came back to report that the road was full of vehicles, and troops were being stationed on all the heights from which observation could be kept. But Grivas had to cross that road, for it was the only way out. Early in the evening he decided to risk it, each man making a dash, one after the other. And they all got across. As he himself went, Grivas saw fresh footprints and an empty English cigarette packet which had only recently been thrown down.

In fact, the British had only a general idea of where Grivas was, and it was almost by chance that, the following night, a patrol of a corporal and four men bumped into him. The patrol had slid down a steep mountainside to come out above a small, isolated religious building— a wayside chapel—in a valley. From this building four or five men rushed, firing as they ran off down the valley. The British patrol followed, but could not keep up in the darkness.

At about four o'clock next afternoon a patrol in a neighbouring valley, led by a sergeant of the Parachute Regiment, spotted the head and shoulders of a man peering over the further ridge. This was in fact Grivas's sentry. The patrol raced down the valley and up the ridge, and were just in time to see four men, who had been resting and washing in a stream, running in alarm for the woods. The patrol opened fire, but did not score a hit, and the men got away. They had left behind them,

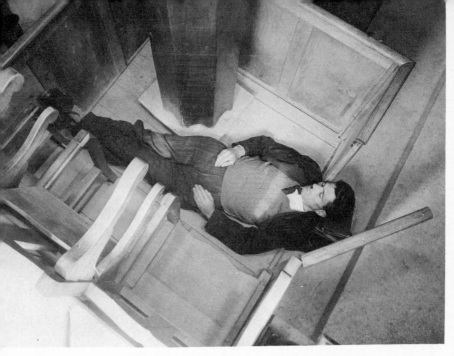

The reality of terror. Four masked men stalked into a church during Sunday morning service and shot a chorister in the back. He lies in the pew where he died.

The reality of terror. Drosoulla Demitriades went happily to a lunch-time meeting with her fiancé in Nicosia. He lay beneath a blanket on the roadway at their meeting place, shot in the back. The girl, flown to England, broadcast a passionate denunciation of Grivas.

The hideout. On mountainsides, in woods, in fields throughout Cyprus, hundreds of underground rooms were dug. They had tiny, well-hidden entrances, such as this one near Paphos. Most were never found.

Since nearly all Greeks in Cyprus were on Grivas's side, anyone could be a terrorist, and general searches for concealed weapons and explosives were part of the British troops' routine.

by the stream, some of their weapons, binoculars, a cardigan, a Sam Browne belt, a beret with grey hairs on it, some reading spectacles in a case made by an Athens oculist, a windproof jacket, shaving kit, and a number of documents, some of which proved to be part of Grivas's diary, made up to the date of 9 June. It had been only a matter of seconds, and of luck, or Grivas himself would have been killed or captured that evening before he could get to the woods.

Now, of course, the search could be concentrated. An area of twenty-five square miles was cordoned, turned into a killing zone, and rigorously patrolled. At dusk the patrols were withdrawn and ambushes were laid inside the cordon. This was the regular drill. It proved most effective except at dusk and dawn, when the ambushes were moving out and back, and cordon troops were nervous of firing in case, in the confusion, they hit their comrades. This operation yielded the capture of another mountain gang led by two £5,000 terrorists, who were hiding in slit trenches, and gave themselves up without a fight, and in a mood of acute depression. But it did not succeed in catching Drakos, who probably slipped out with a couple of companions on the second or third night. Nor did it succeed in catching Grivas himself, though he was still within the area of the cordon on 17 June, and once again nearly trapped. He was moving with three other men along a small path running parallel to the main road along which British motorized forces were passing. Suddenly a few troops turned to the right off the main road into the fields—looking, in fact, for a water-point nearby—and came directly upon them. Grivas took a chance that the troops would mistake him and his companions for peasants; he casually saluted, and the four of them walked steadily on along the path. The troops did not recognize them, and let them go by. When, however, they rejoined their main body, and reported that they had seen four peasants, an officer hastily questioned them, realized what had happened, and immediately switched the search in the direction the four men had taken. This was done so quickly that Grivas had now only a slight lead. He and his men had got into a wooded district, but there was no prepared hide in which they could go to earth. The searchers were now concentrating all round Grivas.

To save himself, he set fire to a patch of forest behind him. The fire burned down one side of a valley and was stopped at a mountain stream, beyond which were stationed a number of troops. There was a sudden freak change in the wind (which, of course, Grivas could not have foreseen). The flames leaped the stream and raced through the dry trees up the opposite slope at a speed of some thirty miles per hour. Nineteen soldiers, most of them trapped in a lorry, were killed, and a further eighteen were injured, of whom one later died. Helicopters came to carry away the injured to hospital. Nothing more was seen in that area of Grivas, who had at last got out of encirclement and was away into a hide where he would not be discovered. It would be two years before he was again in such imminent risk of capture.

In the following weeks he was often out of touch with Nicosia for long periods, but he got some letters through, including one which he sent to his conspirators in Athens, in which he informed them that there was no possibility that he would fail, and that he would fight on, against no matter what odds, and would win. He added that he had never in his life felt so fit, and, with the exception of an occasional bout of diarrhoea, in such perfect health.

While their chief was being harried through the mountains, and in the immediately following period when he was often out of touch, and the organization of the mountain gangs had been largely destroyed, the E.O.K.A. gunmen in the towns tried to create diversions by a series of murders or attempted murders of peculiar unpleasantness. They have only to be related in outline for their savour to be clear.

On 16 May 1956, Corporal T. J. Hale of the R.A.F. was on duty with another N.C.O. in a hut on the edge of Nicosia Airport. There were three Cypriots nearby, cutting corn. Three times they came to the hut to ask for a drink of water, and on each occasion Corporal Hale took water out to them. As he re-entered the hut on the third occasion there was a volley of shots, which killed him. Nearby troops chased and caught the three men, one of them from up a tree. Two were convicted of Corporal Hale's murder, and hanged.

On 3 June, Roy Garrett, the eighteen-year-old son of a British soldier, went for a bathe with two soldiers near their camp at Dhekelia. On the way back they were ambushed by two E.O.K.A. gunmen, who killed one of the soldiers, though the other escaped. They captured the youth, tied his hands behind his back, and shot him in the back. He was not, in fact, dead, but he pretended to be, and the gunmen went away. Four other Cypriots who passed by ignored his cries for help, but he managed to crawl to a nearby church, and was at last discovered, still alive.

On 8 July a Customs official and his wife, Mr. and Mrs. George Kaberry, went for a picnic near the seaside holiday town of Kyrenia. They were ambushed at a road corner in the hills behind the coast, and fired upon with automatic weapons from close range. Mrs. Kaberry, who was pregnant, was killed outright. Her wounded husband was dragged from his car, beaten severely, and then killed by a shotgun fired at point-blank range into his stomach.

On 25 June a Maltese shopkeeper named Mompalda, who was also a special constable in Nicosia, was on his way to a lunch-hour meeting with his fiancée. Just before he met her he was shot in the back five times, and the photograph of the girl in a striped dress sitting on the pavement staring in despair at the dead body of her fiancé was one of the most pathetic of the Cyprus emergency. The girl, Drosoulla Demetriades, was flown to Britain, whence she broadcast a bitter attack on Grivas and urged him to get out of the peaceful island of Cyprus.

In addition to these special murders there was the customary number of killings by bomb and mine, and by shooting in the back in coffee-bar or crowded street.

But these killings were, nevertheless, no more than the continuation of the policy which Grivas had laid down before he was attacked in the Troodos Mountains. They could go on with or without his personal contact. As he came back into touch with his organization, however, and discovered the extent of the losses it had suffered during May and June, he realized that it was on the point of exhaustion, and would have to have a period of rest in order to rebuild itself, or it might be eliminated entirely.

He therefore used an obvious device which he was to try again later. By means of a pamphlet, which the

Government allowed the Cypriots to read without penalty, Grivas offered, in the middle of August, to suspend the campaign of terrorism in order to pave the way for the two sides to come together. The pamphlet was couched in his familiar style: 'For sixteen months the heroic children of Cyprus have been fighting a bitter struggle for freedom. . . .' But what it meant, of course, was that he wanted a breather. This was so patent, following the operations in the mountains, that Sir John Harding in reply merely offered the terrorists the chance to surrender with their arms within three weeks; they could either then go to Greece without trial or remain in Cyprus and face trial. Angered at having his bluff called, Grivas ended his offer for suspension of hostilities with a neat classical allusion. 'My reply to the Government's surrender terms', he announced in his next pamphlet, 'is: "No, come and take it." ' These were the words used at Thermopylae.

Nevertheless, Grivas knew he was on the verge of defeat unless he could gain a pause to regroup his headquarters and his mountain gangs. And here he had one of his usual strokes of luck. This was the year of crisis in the Middle East, when President Nasser nationalized the Suez Canal, the Israel-Egypt War flared out again, and the British made the ill-fated sally into Egypt. It was, of course, precisely as a military base for such eventualities that the British wished to retain the island of Cyprus at all, and it was through Cyprus that the operations were mounted. Grivas tried to interfere with them by E.O.K.A. action, but without any success. How they did benefit him was by withdrawing primary British attention from E.O.K.A. in the mountains. In particular, the mobile striking force of Parachutists had to be taken off internal security duties altogether. Grivas was able, therefore, to devote August and September very largely to reorganization and regrouping, and to increasing as quickly as possible the number of prepared hides, not only in the mountains and the flat countryside, but especially in the towns and villages.

He was helped in his reorganization by the escape from captivity of several of his gang leaders who had been prisoners earlier in the year. Two of them were pulled out of Nicosia General Hospital, where they had been taken for X-ray treatment, on the last day of August. As they were being escorted by police into the hospital, E.O.K.A. staged a well-managed ambush, and a gun battle broke out in which a British police sergeant, a Greek hospital steward, and two of the terrorists were shot dead. But the two important prisoners got away. One of them was Polykarpos Georghiades, a former clerk in the Nicosia Chamber of Commerce, who had been one of the first men whom Grivas recruited. Georghiades had already been taken prisoner once before, and detained in the twelfth-century castle that faces the sea by the side of Kyrenia's little harbour. He escaped from the castle by contriving to get through a narrow window in its ancient walls, and to lower himself on knotted blankets to the rocks below. He then took to the eastern section of the Troodos Mountains, joining the gang of Afxentiou, which had not as yet been very much troubled by British Army operations, since it was established well away from the area in which Grivas kept his headquarters. Georghiades was the luckiest of Grivas's principal lieutenants in his ability to survive the shooting.

While Grivas was thus recuperating his stricken force,

he put up a cover operation against the troops and police, consisting largely of ambushes and bombing attacks, most of which failed because they were not strongly pressed home; but some, of course, caused casualties.

His chief concern, however, was to rebuild the prestige of E.O.K.A. among the general public of Cyprus; it had been severely undermined by the number of gangs which had been mopped up in the mountains during May and June, and by the lack of fight they had shown, and their obviously poor morale. Unless he could command the support of the Cypriot Greek population, Grivas would be lost; already, at these signs of his weakness, the flow of information to reach the British from the general public had remarkably increased.

The means by which he could regain public support were more limited now than they had been. For example, Grivas no longer had the same grip on the school-children. In the previous school year, secondary education in the island had been brought practically to a standstill. This was causing a good deal of disquiet to the parents, and Grivas, who never for a moment forgot that basically he was fighting a battle of propaganda, eased up on his incitement of the children to indiscipline. During the summer holidays, too, the Government at last dealt with teachers who were Greek nationals, recruited from Greece—there were more than 100 of them—who had been the most extreme in provoking their pupils to violence, or, indeed, sharing in it with them. One was caught helping the boys of his class to mine a road-bridge; another gave his pupils regular instruction in the use of arms. So all except seven were either turned out of Cyprus by having their residence permits refused, or themselves returned voluntarily to their own country. School life in Cyprus began to get back to something like normal.

Moreover, the use of youngsters by E.O.K.A. out of school hours was not as popular with their parents, or quite as readily tolerated, as it had been. It was at this time that stories of sexual immorality between the E.O.K.A. youths and young girls began to circulate in this island where family life is, normally, strictly controlled by the parents, and any such laxity outside marriage or the promise of marriage most rigorously condemned. From the very beginning Grivas had been worried by the difficulties that would follow from recruiting girls into his organization. There were, of course, the obvious security risks, and, to minimize those, he strove at one time to keep his mountain-gang members celibate, or at least to forbid them to form any new liaisons. These instructions were less carefully observed than most which Grivas issued, and he uneasily issued fresh orders that E.O.K.A. was not to be regarded as an excuse for sexual immorality, but was to be treated always as 'a serious business'.

He did contemplate various sensational activities which would help restore his prestige. There was a meeting in the mountain village of Milikouri, not far from Kykko Monastery, with several of his gang leaders, at which possible operations of this kind were discussed. One suggestion put forward was that British children—particularly those of the Service families in the island—should be abducted. To this, Grivas was not altogether opposed. Then it was suggested that British women should be seized for long enough for their heads to be shaved, and should then be released to their homes. At this suggestion Grivas flew into a rage. He said that he would not stoop to such acts, and gave stern orders that they were never again to be contemplated.

His curious reaction to these two suggestions—possible consent to the abduction of children, but repugnance at shaving women's heads—seems inexplicable until it is remembered that he was basing his campaign on a study of guerrilla activity in Greece during and after the occupation. That was what conditioned his thinking. There had been in Greece no petty shaving of women's heads, but during the civil war the Communists had abducted thousands of Greek children, taking them over the northern frontiers to hold them as hostages against the Greek Army. To Grivas, therefore, this latter operation seemed a permissible and natural way of conducting a guerrilla campaign. That he did not put it into effect was because he had not the organization to do so.

There was in fact one abduction at this time, not of a child, but of a retired civil servant named Jack Cramer, who was seventy-eight years of age, and who lived in Kyrenia. He had been to the nearby Turkish village of Templos to give English lessons to some schoolgirls. As he was returning home at dusk, four masked men got out of a car, blindfolded and gagged him, took him he knew not where, and kept him tied up and gagged for three days. Three young E.O.K.A. terrorists named Zakos, Michael and Patatsos were in gaol and due to be hanged, and there was an E.O.K.A. announcement that if they were executed, Cramer would be shot. There was an over-dramatic appeal from the three convicts themselves to E.O.K.A. not to harm the old man, which led the British to suspect that the whole thing was a job put up for the purpose of allowing the melodramatic appeal to be made. At last Cramer was taken by car and deposited early in the morning on the doorstep of his house, where he soon recovered from the shock, and at the end of the emergency was still living happily.

Grivas did not order this abduction, and was not consulted about it. Not only was he at that time having difficulties with his system of couriers, but there was also some indiscipline among his own men, particularly those who were at a distance from him. The Kyrenia group who seized the old man fully intended to shoot him if the three convicts were hanged (as, a few days later, they were). They were dissuaded from doing so by members of the Church, who were growing ever more uneasy at the state of public opinion and feared that shooting such an aged man might have a serious effect on it. During the exile of the Archbishop, it was the Bishop of Kitium who probably wielded the greatest influence with the terrorists; later in the same month he was placed under house arrest.

One method remained by which Grivas could re-establish his hold over the Cypriot Greek public, and check the flow of information which was reaching the British Intelligence organization. That was the original method of terror. And this he put into operation. During the last six months of 1956, E.O.K.A. murders of Greek civilians were incessant, and at the end of the year reached their peak. Day after day, in the towns and to a lesser extent in the villages, a revolver shot rang out, the youth who had fired ducked into the back streets, everybody in the vicinity hurried away, nobody had seen or heard anything when the police arrived; and one more body lay in its blood on the hot tarmac of the road, or slumped across the table of a coffee-shop. A few of the victims were British soldiers, airmen, police or civilians. The meanest murder of all was that of Dr. Charles Bevan at Limassol. Dr. Bevan had served the Cypriot people for twenty years as a physician, and had played a leading part in the establishment of preventive medicine in the island, particularly for tuberculosis. Two E.O.K.A. men entered the hospital, one saying that he needed medical attention. As Dr. Bevan examined him, the other man shot him in the back. Then they both ran away.

But most of the E.O.K.A. victims were Greeks. From July until the end of the year, sixty-six Greeks were murdered by E.O.K.A. A few of them were killed by chance when bombs were thrown at vehicles. Most were deliberately shot in the street, or in shops, offices and coffee-houses. One man was shot at a wedding ceremony, another in the house of a friend on whom he was making a call, and another in his own bed. Two of them were taken into one of the main streets of Nicosia with their hands tied, and were shot in the back in full public view.

None of this shooting was indiscriminate. Every murder was ordered, or at the least sanctioned, by Grivas personally. He had returned to his mountain hideouts, where he could live in security once more, since the main effort of the British troops had been diverted to the Middle East situation. Requests to shoot named people came to him from various functionaries in his district organizations, sometimes from the political side of it, known as P.E.K.A. Grivas considered each case and, if the man was to be shot, sent a message to that effect to the leader of the local killer group, who then carried out the murder, either himself or through one of his few reliable assassins, without further question. The murderer needed to know no more about his victim than the fact that Grivas had ordered him to be killed.

The purpose of the intensive slaughter of Greeks during the latter six months of 1956 was to re-establish by terror the E.O.K.A. grip on the civilian population, and to choke back information that might have gone to the security forces. The pretext for each killing was that the man was a traitor. But most of the people who were killed were quite unknown to the British or to the police as informers. Grivas's definition of treachery was a very loose one. It could be stretched to include an expression of disapproval of E.O.K.A. It certainly included disobedience to, or even intended disregard of, Grivas's orders or personal wishes. If, for example, a shopkeeper did not close his shop when instructed to by E.O.K.A., his first punishment was likely to be a beating-up; for a second offence, he would be shot in the back. It was vital for Grivas to make known to the Greek public that any flouting of his rule, or any hint of collaboration with the British, would be followed by death. As he warned his first recruits in the earliest days of his campaign, 'I will shoot anybody who disobeys me. I am not playing.'

Take the case of Andreas Lazarou, who was a watchmaker in Nicosia, where he had a prosperous business, a wife named Stavroulla, and six children. Soon after Grivas had been smuggled into Cyprus in 1954, an acquaintance warned Lazarou that his name was high on the list for execution, because during the World War he had served in the British Army. He was told, however, that he could save his life, and the happiness of his family, if he joined E.O.K.A. Under such pressure, he joined. He was given the code name of Praktoras, and his shop became one of the post-boxes in Nicosia for the delivery and collection of letters and messages to and from Grivas in the mountains. Once he was in E.O.K.A., Lazarou got more and more deeply involved. He found himself driving lorries in which explosives and ammunition were hidden. Twice he made journeys of that kind to the Troodos Mountains, and he was so trusted that once he had lunch with Grivas himself.

Lazarou's wife, Stavroulla, fell ill, and early in 1956 she went to Greece for medical examination, where she was found to have an inoperable cancer. The medical expenses, and the cost of the journey to Greece, had put Lazarou heavily in debt, and he could see no way of continuing to support his family in Nicosia. He knew, however, that if he sold his business and went to London, he could get well-paid employment as a skilled watchmaker. It happened that at the same time his father lay dying, so that the family ties in Cyprus would soon be still further loosened.

It is indicative of the hold that Grivas had over these people that Lazarou did not simply arrange to go to London, but wrote to Grivas asking for his permission to do so. He wrote the letter on a Monday early in September 1956, and gave it to one of the messengers who was going to Grivas's central command post. On the Friday morning a messenger returned with a verbal message that Lazarou was to be in his shop that afternoon, when he would receive Grivas's reply. His brother called that day and wanted Lazarou to accompany him to their father's bedside, since he was sinking fast, but Lazarou decided he had better obey the order of 'the old man' (or 'uncle', as E.O.K.A. members often referred to Grivas in conversation, though in any more formal communication he was always Dighenis, or Leader).

Lazarou therefore remained in his shop until 4.20 p.m., when he received Grivas's reply. A passing gunman shot him dead through the open window.

Who were these few gunmen, never more than perhaps forty or fifty of them, with whom Grivas terrorized half a million people?

They were all very young. Grivas's study of Communist experience in Greece had convinced him that only from youths in their late teens or early twenties can assassins be moulded who will kill on order, and without question, and he proved the accuracy of this in Cyprus. All of the first nine terrorists who, after trial, conviction and appeal, were hanged, were between nineteen and twenty-three years of age.

They had to be young, because they had to have a combination of youthful daring and fanatical conviction, indoctrinated into them, that they were behaving in a heroic way. These boys—most of them were little more— were not criminals by nature or instinct. They had to be corrupted, and to be convinced that what they did was not a crime, but an act of bravery. To understand the hold that Grivas was able to fix on them, it is necessary to realize that they genuinely regarded themselves as heroic, that they were so regarded by a great many of their fellow-countrymen, and that Grivas himself, for all the deliberation of his plan, was self-deluded into a fanatical belief that his struggle was just and heroic, not only in its aims, but in its methods.

The way in which schoolboys were gradually brought to the point of committing assassinations is clearly seen in the story of one of those who were hanged, Evagoras Pallikarides. He came from the village of Tsadha, in the foothills above Ktima, at the south-western corner of

Cyprus. His father was a police sergeant at Ktima, and young Pallikarides went to school at the gymnasium at nearby Paphos, one of the most riotous schools in the island. When Grivas arrived in Cyprus to begin his campaign of terrorism, Pallikarides was sixteen years old, and he took the E.O.K.A. oath while he was still at school.

On his first conviction, for taking part in the riot at Paphos when Loizides and the gun-runners were being tried, he was fined £10. From there he graduated, in spite of his father's pleading, to masked attacks on Government buildings with explosives. As a reward, he was given a trip to Greece during his summer holidays in 1955, and he smuggled an automatic weapon back with him.

When he returned to school in the autumn, he was deeply embroiled in E.O.K.A., not only as a leaflet-distributor, but as a bomb-thrower. He was arrested as a ringleader of a schoolchildren's riot. He jumped his bail and made for the mountains, where he joined a gang in a hideout at Pano Panayia, on the southern slopes of the range. It was this gang, at that time, which murdered the Abbot of the nearby monastery of Chrysoroyiatissa, who was wrongly thought to have betrayed two E.O.K.A men to the British. Pallikarides's group took part in an ineffectual attack on a police station, and funked at the last minute an assault on a military camp. After a few weeks with the schoolboy bomb-throwers of Nicosia, Pallikarides went back to the mountains, and joined a gang hiding up near the village of Lyso, at the western end of the island. This time he took part in a raid on a military camp, and in an ambush, which failed, of a military vehicle. It was then that the troops started flushing E.O.K.A. out of his section of the mountains, and the group was on the run from hide to hide. It is probable that they would have been arrested and broken up, had not the Suez crisis diverted the troops elsewhere.

Now he was sufficiently indoctrinated. In November his district commander gave him a 0·38 revolver, and told him to execute a sixty-year-old villager in Lyso named Tomazos, who was said to collaborate with a Turkish policeman. Pallikarides went to the village, said he was a messenger from the Army, and told Tomazos that an officer wished to speak to him; he also told the villagers to go and stock their houses with food and water, since next day there would be a curfew.

Tomazos went with Pallikarides outside the village, and then the boy told him, 'I have orders to execute you because you are a traitor. We have information that you collaborate with a Turkish policeman, who will also be executed.'

The old man pleaded that he was no traitor, the Turk was simply a friend of his, and begged for pity. The boy offered to give him time to say his prayers, then shot him in the left side. The old man fell. Pallikarides fired three more shots, nervously and wildly. Only one hit Tomazos, in the right temple, and did not kill him. The boy then nerved himself to go right up to the old man, to whom he said, 'Forgive me, if you wish,' before shooting him through the head.

Security forces were now again moving through that part of the mountains, and the gang to which Pallikarides belonged moved to a different part, where they would construct themselves a hide in which to spend the winter. Pallikarides set out at night with two donkeys, carrying a Bren gun, and was caught by a passing patrol. In March 1957, after trial, conviction and appeal, he was hanged.

Young children, as well as their older brothers, were cynically brought into the struggle by E.O.K.A. It was from behind this screen of children that, at a village near Nicosia, a gunman had just opened fire on a British troops convoy.

The reality of terror. Three British policemen, walking in Nicosia's Ledra Street—'Murder Mile'—were shot from behind by terrorists. Two lie dead. The third, wounded, turns to fire after the fleeing assassins. Passing Cypriots hurry by. Nobody offers to help.

Grivas (third from right) with his personal gang of terrorists in the Cypriot mountains. Markos Drakos is second from the left. This photograph was found during mountain operations of 1956..

The campaign is over. Grivas returns to triumph in Athens. He and his wife are welcomed by the Greek Prime Minister, Constantine Karamanlis.

It is possible to see enough of the fanatical indoctrination to have still a little pity for this boy who was persuaded to carry out such a cold-blooded murder while he was only eighteen years old. But for some other members of the killer groups it is difficult to feel anything but repugnance. There was one young journalist and photographer, aged only twenty-one, who was often the first on the scene after a shooting in Ledra Street or elsewhere in Nicosia, and was found photographing the body for the newspapers. Although, for lack of corroborative evidence, no murder was ever pinned on him, it became known later that he himself had shot the victims. His method was to be followed down the street by two or three young girls. When he had picked out a man to kill—and it is suspected that about a dozen of his victims were British—he shot him in the back, threw the revolver to one of the girls, who popped it into her handbag and vanished with it, and then the journalist proceeded to take photographs of the body. Of all Grivas's young assassins, this was the most detested.

CHAPTER XII

THE BRITISH were now, however, preparing to take the initiative on three fronts.

The first was the political front. During 1956 Lord Radcliffe had been appointed Constitutional Commissioner for Cyprus, had visited the island twice—though Greek Cypriot representatives refused to speak to him—and in December published his proposed Constitution for the island. It offered the Greek Cypriots self-government in all matters except foreign affairs, defence and internal security, while safe-guarding the Turkish minority. At the same time the Colonial Secretary announced in the House of Commons that, once the strategic situation permitted, and if self-government were working well, the question of self-determination, for which the Greeks had so long struggled, would be reviewed. He warned, however, that it might entail partition of the island, since the Turkish Cypriots, as well as the Greek, would also be entitled to decide under what rule they wished to live.

The second was the international front. Greece was once again urging that the General Assembly of the United Nations should discuss the question of self-determination for Cyprus. The British Government now asked the General Assembly to consider a complaint that Greece was supporting terrorism in Cyprus.

The third front was that of military operations against E.O.K.A. wherever terrorism was operating. Once the

Suez crisis had passed, the Army was again available for full-scale hunting down of E.O.K.A.—it was always hunting rather than fighting—and it was clear that the terrorists would have to be cleaned up, not only in the mountains, from which they were making sallies and ambushes against camps and military vehicles, but also in the towns, where the campaign of murder had reached its peak. The commander of these operations against Grivas and his men was Major-General D. A. Kendrew.

The operation started at a strong disadvantage to the British, since the E.O.K.A. recovery in the mountains and the intensified campaign of murder in the towns had closed most sources of information. But General Kendrew now had a considerably reinforced mobile striking force, and a larger number of R.A.F. helicopters whose pilots had learned to overcome the considerable technical difficulties of operating over steep mountain slopes. They had learned, for instance, that even in a descent of 25 feet the wind could veer through 180 degrees; the first helicopter to discover this hit Mount Olympus at a height of 6,000 feet and slid a long way down a steep slope, smashing its rotor blades, before coming to rest.

In the last few weeks of 1956 the military sweeps were made in the north of the island, and in the early days of the new year the area moved westwards to the Troodos Range, where most of the reconstructed mountain gangs were then established, and where Grivas himself was in deep hiding. By establishing close cordons, and setting ambushes inside them at night, the security forces soon began to flush out members of the gangs. Their first big success came on 18 January. The weather was severe, and the mountains were drenched with heavy rainstorms that followed violent outbreaks of thunder. At midnight a patrol of the Suffolk Regiment were setting an ambush near Troodos itself when they suddenly saw two terrorists at close range. Neither side had suspected the other's presence until this sudden encounter. One of the terrorists got in the first burst of fire, but hit nobody, and the return fire killed him. He was Markos Drakos, who, after Afxentiou, was Grivas's most successful terrorist, and closest in his confidence. Drakos, a short, slim young man with a serious face—he was only twenty-four when he was killed—had carried out the most successful of the sabotage attacks with which the campaign opened on 1 April 1955. He had been near to Grivas in the mountain operations of the following year, had lain up within gunshot of him throughout, moving southward with him as a kind of bodyguard, and had been one of the few mountain gang leaders to avoid capture at that time.

His death made a considerable difference to the security operations. Schoolchildren went on strike to mourn him, and Athens Radio broadcast an elegy for 'the terror of the British, and beloved of the gods . . . All Cypriot children should try to be like him. Troodos is in silence; not even the birds are singing.' But the more calculating people in Cyprus reckoned that the death of Markos Drakos was a sign that the British would soon be on top again, and information began to be received of a higher quality than at any previous time.

As a result, the E.O.K.A. town gangs were virtually cleaned up during the first three months of 1957. In Nicosia two British civilians were shot in January, and a gallant Greek police constable died after chasing the men who had shot him. Two more Britons were shot in Famagusta, and a Turkish policeman was killed by a bomb. Then the murders in the towns died away for a year. Even the slaughter of Greek Cypriots, which had been so appalling during the latter half of 1956, diminished rapidly in January and February of the New Year, and ended in March, as the police and troops, provided with ever more and more information, unearthed the weapons and explosives hidden in the towns, and swept members of the town gangs into prison.

Seeing all this, the local E.O.K.A. gangs in the villages quietly cached their arms and drifted back into normal life.

In smashing the town gangs, the security forces secured another of Grivas's closest associates, a young journalist named Nicos Sampson, who had suddenly vanished from Nicosia, where he was well known, and had therefore drawn suspicion on himself as having been implicated in several murders in the centre and the suburbs of Nicosia. Sampson's hiding-place was given away by an informer. Shortly after midnight on 30 January a dozen plain-clothes policemen entered a house in Dhali, a village twelve miles south of Nicosia, and found Sampson in possession of a Sten gun and ammunition. After his arrest he was driven in an open vehicle for forty minutes on a wet night without his shoes and socks, was not provided with a change of clothing at the police station, but only with an electric fire and two blankets, and was not given (and does not seem to have needed or requested) medical attention for any injuries he sustained when being arrested. He made a very long statement to the police, and was charged with murder. At his trial, however, strong allegations of deliberate torture and brutality, based on the treatment outlined above, were made by the defence. The judge stated categorically that he entirely disbelieved these allegations, but he refused to admit as evidence the statement that Sampson had made to the police, as there was some doubt in his mind as to whether it was made entirely voluntarily. In the event, Sampson was convicted of being in possession of a weapon, a capital offence under the Emergency Regulations, and was condemned to death. Since he had not been convicted of an actual murder, he was reprieved, and the sentence commuted to imprisonment.

Early in March, Grivas received perhaps the severest personal blow of the campaign. An operation was mounted in the Makheras Forest, around the Makheras Monastery, in which area his second in command, Gregorios Afxentiou, had been established for some nine months, and where he had avoided the most intensive military searches of the previous year.

Now, however, it was his turn. Soon after the operation began, fifteen terrorists were picked up and several machine guns and a lot of ammunition were discovered. As always, success in capturing some of the terrorists released information about others. On 2 March, troops had pinpointed a hide on the mountainside only half a mile from the monastery, in which five terrorists were trapped. When the hide was surrounded, and the men realized they were cornered, they opened fire, and in the short gun battle that followed, one of the British troops was killed. A short time afterwards, seeing that the position was hopeless, four of the terrorists came out and surrendered. One of them was a leading E.O.K.A. man, Antonis Papadopoulos, who had been with Grivas from the start, and on whose head was a price of £5,000. The fifth man, who had remained inside, was now known to be Afxentiou himself.

One of the other terrorists, named Matrosis, was sent back into the hide to try to persuade Afxentiou to give himself up. The British waited for some time, calling upon the two men to show themselves, but neither appeared. Charges were therefore applied to the entrance to the hide. Some time after they had been fired, Matrosis came out again and surrendered. Afxentiou lay inside, dead. There are some grounds for thinking that he had shot himself.

At that moment, E.O.K.A. was virtually crushed. It was practically stripped clean of its organization in the towns and villages. The worst of the assassins had been captured. More than sixty E.O.K.A. men were in gaol facing capital charges. The mountain gangs had nearly all been broken up, and deprived of their leaders, and Grivas's two chief lieutenants had been killed. If the operations had been continued rather longer, and Grivas himself could have been taken at that time in the mountains, the whole Cyprus rebellion would have collapsed, and peace would have returned to the island.

But the operations were not continued sufficiently long, and Grivas was not caught. He now drew a dividend from the propaganda war which he had waged in the past. The terrorist campaign had been conducted from the first with the basic aim of influencing world opinion and by that method forcing Britain to hand over Cyprus to Greece. It had so far succeeded that in February 1957 the United Nations General Assembly, which had twice refused to discuss the Cyprus question, now heard, in its Political Committee, the Greek application for self-determination for Cyprus, and the British complaint that Greece had supported terrorism. In the end a somewhat innocuous resolution, proposed as a compromise by

India, was approved, expressing an earnest desire for a peaceful, democratic and just solution, and a hope that negotiations would be resumed to that end. Shortly afterwards the Secretary-General of N.A.T.O. offered to act as mediator between Greece and Turkey in the dispute which was growing in bitterness and so threatened the structure of N.A.T.O.

All this gave Grivas the chance that he wanted. He issued a leaflet which offered to suspend violence as soon as Archbishop Makarios was set free. And the Archbishop was freed at the end of the month, since he made some sort of conciliatory statement, though not the outright condemnation of violence for which he had been asked. He was released from the Seychelles, but was not, of course, permitted to return to Cyprus. He went therefore to Athens, and was received by the family of Valvis, the lawyer who had been Grivas's associate and had played a large part in launching the terrorist campaign. The Archbishop also at once resumed contact with Andreas Azinas, the former Reading University student, who had been his chief liaison with Grivas in the early days in Cyprus, had fled to Athens when the gun-running *caique* was about to be captured, and had been Grivas's principal representative in Athens ever since.

Grivas therefore called his 'truce' and the British accepted it. It cheated them of the operational success they were on the point of achieving, but it is difficult to see what else they could have done. To have rejected it in the face of the United Nations resolution would have had precisely the effect on world public opinion that Grivas was striving all the time to create. His assessment of the situation was logical and correct, and he used it with the most skilful timing to extricate himself from the defeat into which General Kendrew's operations had nearly thrust him.

Sir John Harding's appreciation of the position was, of course, just as accurate, as Grivas fully realized. Sir John knew that E.O.K.A. was almost knocked out, but that Grivas intended to rebuild and reorganize. He also knew that it would take him at least three months, and probably more, to do so. The question was how much Sir John could do to prevent Grivas getting operational again, without wrecking other chances of a political settlement, which now seemed somewhat brighter. The answer was that, apart from searching for arms and continuing to build up the Intelligence service of the security forces, he could do very little. If Grivas could recruit new E.O.K.A. leaders, and find sufficient with which to arm them, he might yet harry Britain into something near a political surrender; though already it was becoming clear that the one factor with which Grivas could not hope to deal, the Turkish factor, was growing in importance.

CHAPTER XIII

WHEN Archbishop Makarios was freed from the Seychelles, and Grivas from his hideout tendered a suspension of operations—ostensibly as a pacific gesture, actually because E.O.K.A. was on its knees— the Governor offered a safe conduct out of Cyprus to Grivas and to any other foreign nationals who were members of E.O.K.A. and were still at large. An Auster aircraft was sent loud-hailing the offer over the mountains. But there was no reply from Grivas, or from any other hidden E.O.K.A. men. Sir John Harding, in an endeavour to facilitate a political settlement, relaxed many of the Emergency Regulations. Still there was silence from the mountains. Day followed day, and week followed week, and Grivas made no move and no announcement. For more than fifty days nothing was heard from him.

What he was doing, in addition to starting the reorganization of his stricken E.O.K.A., was waiting instructions from Archbishop Makarios, who was himself waiting to see whether the British Government would continue to regard the United Nations resolution as calling for talks only between the three Governments, or whether he himself would be included. When he was not, he sent Grivas a message to refuse the safe conduct and to remain in Cyprus at the ready.

One activity which Sir John Harding's forces kept up during the long 'truce' in 1957 was the search for hidden weapons, ammunition and explosives. They found much, even though arms and explosives had been hauled in from all parts of the island continuously for some two years. In the month following Grivas's leaflet offering to suspend operations, for instance, security forces unearthed a large cache of explosives at the village of Pano Amiandos, a dozen pistols and shotguns from various parts of the island, and two arsenals at Avgorou and Lefka, which give a good idea of the reserves of arms and explosives which were still available to Grivas.

At Avgorou were found 11 shotguns, 1 rifle, 2 pistols, 9 live bombs, 3 mortar bombs, 2 live 3·7 shells, 1 rifle magazine, 3 Sten-gun magazines, 1 large bomb prepared for detonation, 300 percussion caps, 1 time pencil, 129 live rounds of various calibres, a large bag of shot, 2 electric detonators, 2 jars of gunpowder, and 3 large batteries wired for detonation. At Lefka a patrol captured seven wanted men, who had in their hideout 2 Thompson submachine guns, 1 Sten gun, 3 shotguns, 1 Italian carbine, 1 American fragmentation bomb, nearly 400 rounds of ammunition, 72 cartridges, 3 time pencils, 45 mixed electric and commercial detonators, 6 Thompson magazines and 3 Sten-gun magazines.

Hoards of this kind were discovered almost every week. Within the year following the opening of the Grivas truce, security forces captured 95 pistols or revolvers, 9 submachine guns, 9 rifles, 1 mortar, 61 shotguns, 6 home-made guns (fearfully dangerous weapons to the firers), 28 magazines, 15 mines, 506 sticks of dynamite, 240 bombs and grenades, 2,814 shotgun cartridges and 3,196 rounds of ammunition. But these were only a small fraction of the weapons and explosives which E.O.K.A. still had hidden away.

Moreover, Grivas had two sources from which he could always count on replenishing his arsenals. One was the smuggling of arms from Greece. The other was manufacture of crude weapons from material that was available on the island.

Smuggling of arms, ammunition and explosives into Cyprus began long before the campaign of terrorism started, and continued throughout its course, in spite of all the authorities could do. It started after Grivas's first reconnaissance visit to the island in 1951, and by the time he came secretly in 1954 to get E.O.K.A. under way, considerable quantities of weapons had been landed and cached by his fellow-conspirators in Cyprus. There had also been a well-organized series of thefts of explosives of various kinds from the mines which are worked in the island—chiefly chrome and asbestos mines in the Troodos Mountains—and these explosives had also been hidden away against the day.

After the capture of the *St. George*, the fishing vessel which attempted to run in a big load of weapons and explosives early in 1955, the Navy put a radar and patrol watch around the island which prevented any further smuggling on that scale. Grivas therefore changed his tactics. His assistants in Greece organized a lot of smuggling of weapons in tiny parts. Revolvers were stripped right down into their components and different visitors to Cyprus each brought in one of the parts. Sometimes it would take three weeks before a single whole revolver could be reassembled. For a time, schoolchildren who had been on holiday in Greece succeeded in bringing back weapons in their luggage. Then the device was tried, with quite remarkable success, of sending weapons hidden in parcels which reached Cyprus from Greece by normal mail. A favourite method was to pack them into cases containing school textbooks. This was discovered as early as December 1955, when four such cases from Greece were found to contain two Thompson sub-machine guns, one Sten gun, 2,000 rounds of ammunition, limpet mines, Mills grenades and smoke bombs, all professionally packed in Greece in wrappers bearing the name of the Hellenic Gunpowder and Detonator Manufacturers Limited, Athens.

In spite of the authorities' knowledge of the smuggling of weapons and ammunition through the post, it went on for another couple of years. There were, indeed, a few red faces when a letter addressed to 'E.O.K.A. Organization, Limassol', which arrived in January 1956, was found to contain a circular letter from the Directors and Staff of the arms factory, 'Rigarmi', of Brescia, Italy. The Directors and Staff sent New Year greetings to their business friends, thanked them for their support during the past year, and hoped for the favour of their continued patronage in the future.

The reason that smuggling of arms through the parcel post was able to continue was that there was no adequate organization in Cyprus for the examination of parcels, and it was not until towards the end of the emergency that one was established. It had to be a somewhat elaborate building, with X-ray equipment for examining the parcels, and sandbagged bays fitted with distant-control claw arms for undoing those which, it was suspected, were booby-trapped. However, it was after the parcels-examination service was fully established that some of the biggest supplies of arms were sent by this method. E.O.K.A. had long since penetrated the Civil Service, and the parcels in question were diverted around the examination building by the use of forged and stolen rubber stamps.

One supply of explosives which went for a long time undiscovered was the despatch from Greece of crates of china ornaments in the shape of comic black cats; the sort of thing that is frequently seen on sale in a souvenir shop.

About these black cats, however, there was a difference. They were not made of china, but of solid T.N.T., enamelled over.

Grivas at one time wanted to get arms from Egypt, but was discouraged from doing so. The weapons that were smuggled to him came from Greece. Some of them, such as the time pencils, which were one of the worst enemies of the security forces, were of British origin. This material was smuggled in from Greece with the knowledge, and perhaps the connivance, of Greek authorities; accusations have been made, and denied, that some weapons were carried in the diplomatic bags.

As time went on, however, Grivas was able to supply an ever-increasing proportion of his requirements from materials that were to be had in Cyprus itself. Some of these were relics of the World War, after which large quantities of land-mines were dumped into the sea off Cyprus. Fishermen had from time to time dredged up a few in their nets and found that the explosive could still be used for stunning fish. E.O.K.A. set about dredging up a great many of them. The mines themselves were nearly all unserviceable, but the explosive they contained could be used in other bombs. There were also explosives buried on the island—demolition mines which had been laid at key points after the German capture of Crete, in case of an invasion of Cyprus. Most of them were quietly removed by E.O.K.A. for the sake of the explosives they contained.

On the island, which holds a largely agricultural community, were several thousand shotguns of a sporting type. The Government made an order that they were all to be handed in, and many were secured and stowed away in Kyrenia Castle. But many more were taken by E.O.K.A. schoolchildren, who were told to bicycle hastily round and grab all the shotguns they could before the Government order could be enforced. The cartridge shells were used over and over again. Blacksmiths made crude instruments for refilling them with powder and shot.

Finally, there was one reservoir that seemed unlikely ever to dry up completely. Grivas taught his followers how to make lethal weapons from everyday materials that could be purchased in the shops.

For the manufacture of explosives they used potassium chlorate which, in spite of protests from the Army, was freely on sale in chemists' shops; not until late in the emergency was its supply limited. This chemical, which is used for medical and some agricultural purposes, needs only to be mixed with sugar to produce an explosive which, when detonated in a bomb, will go off with considerable force. Sulphur, which is widely used in Cyprus for spraying vines, was also often added to the mixture, to increase its efficiency.

The bombs and mines into which this explosive was packed were made from such ordinary household objects as tin cans. A smaller can, for example, was placed inside a larger can. The space between the two was filled with bits of old iron, rusty nails, stones and any other sort of shrapnel. The inner can was filled with explosive, in which was a detonator mechanism, fired by a fuse. And the whole, of course, was securely sealed down. The explosion of such a shrapnel bomb could kill a dozen men standing within a few yards of it.

Most of the heavier bombs were made from lengths of ordinary water-pipe, and particularly from water-pipe junctions. The method of manufacture was this. A plumber in one of the towns took a length of pipe, or a junction, from his stock, and fitted all the ends with screwed-in metal caps. He then sent it, seemingly quite innocent plumbing equipment, to the next E.O.K.A. man in the chain, who scored the metal with a saw, so that it would fragment on explosion. This man sent it on to the next in line, who filled it with home-made explosive, inserted a fuse and detonator, and used it. Thousands of these pieces of plumbing travelled about the island, often in the parcels service on the country buses. Some of them, of course, were discovered at road-checks, when the driver professed complete ignorance and innocence—he thought he was merely delivering water-pipes. But most of them got through. Many of the smaller ones, of hand-grenade size, were carried by women and schoolgirls. Even heavy ones were sometimes carried by peasant women riding on donkeys. Since there was a strict rule that women could be searched only by women, the security forces were greatly hampered in their attempts to find and seize these bombs which, towards the end of the terrorism campaign, became E.O.K.A.'s main armoury.

They were used in several ways. Some were small enough to be thrown by hand. Some of the largest were used as pipe mortars. A length of pipe was packed with explosive, then a big load of shrapnel, then wadding. It was fixed by night in a bank by the side of a busy road and aligned on the oncoming headlights of military vehicles. From a detonator in the explosive, two wires were trailed back 600 or 700 yards into the surrounding countryside, where an E.O.K.A. man with an electric battery lay concealed beneath a bush. When a military vehicle carrying soldiers was in line with the pipe mortar, he detonated it electrically, raking the vehicle with shrapnel and often causing several casualties. The E.O.K.A. man ducked back into the forest and was very rarely caught.

Other mines were placed in drainage culverts under tarmac roads and were similarly exploded by electricity from a distance when a vehicle was over the culvert; many of these failed, because to time the explosion was a matter of some difficulty, but many others succeeded in wrecking vehicles and taking lives.

On the lesser roads, which were unpaved, pressure mines of the crudest kind were buried, and they ambushed many vehicles. The mechanism consisted simply of two rough strips of wood, hinged together at one edge and kept apart at the other by a couple of small metal springs. This device was buried just beneath the surface of the road. When a vehicle's weight pressed the two pieces of wood together, the top one depressed an ordinary sixpenny bellpush, which completed the circuit to an electric battery, and detonated the tinful of homemade explosive buried just below. One of these devices even succeeded in blowing up a tank.

The training of bomb-manufacturers and the accumulation of a fresh supply of weapons were two of the main occupations of Grivas during the quieter period of 1957. Another was the recruitment of new leaders to form new groups in all parts of the E.O.K.A. organization—in the mountains, the villages and the towns. It was in the villages that he encountered the greatest reluctance to prepare for another campaign of violence. In the towns he still had fanatical youngsters coming out of school who could be trained as executioners and to whom, even during the so-called truce period, he gave a little practice; twelve people were killed, and eighty-five injured, by E.O.K.A. action while Grivas had formally suspended operations.

The first sign that he was getting his organization back into shape came at the end of June, when a leaflet announced that E.O.K.A. was on the alert. One curiosity is that none of the leaflets at about this time bore Grivas's own signature of 'Dighenis', and neither did they seem to be couched in his own familiar, rhetorical style. There were many rumours that he had succeeded in leaving the island, and had gone to Beirut, from which town he was secretly conducting E.O.K.A. at a distance. There was also a strong rumour that he was hidden for a time in the Greek Consulate in Cyprus. Grivas's intimates in Athens, however, have been assured that he was in Cyprus throughout the four years of E.O.K.A. action, and that he was hiding for about half the time in the mountains, and about half the time in the towns or villages. On one or two occasions he claims to have been very nearly trapped by British troops. One of these was at Spilia, a mountain village on a north-eastern slope of the Troodos Range that is pitted with caves. He was resting in an upstairs room of a house when the village was suddenly filled with troops, who began a house-to-house search. He told a girl who lived in the house to go downstairs, and said that, if the troops came up, he would fight his way out. The girl met the patrol downstairs, offered the troops some coffee, chatted pleasantly with them—an unusual experience on these search operations—and then said, 'And now you'd like to search the house.' But the troops politely told this agreeable young woman that there was no need of that, and cheerfully left.

Grivas was again well hidden in Cyprus, and in strict control of the revived E.O.K.A. by July of 1957. He started to put out more threatening leaflets, and he ordered a series of operations in which he could test out his new leaders before he had got most of them to the pitch of murder. These operations consisted of attacking the village leaders, called *Mukhtars*, and as trophies seizing their seals of office. One of them, the *Mukhtar* of Dahli, who had not been collaborating in any way with the British, was shot dead. At the same time, Grivas ordered the beginnings of a campaign of assault on left-wing Greek Cypriots—not necessarily only Communists, but those who held trade union office—which was an activity always to his liking.

By September he had re-established several mountain gangs and had begun to re-create his killer groups in the towns, though the villages were still proving troublesome. After the virtual destruction of E.O.K.A. in the preceding winter, he knew that he would have to begin the programme again from the beginning, in order to work his followers up to sufficient pitch, and he therefore planned an opening campaign of simple sabotage, in which the first target was to be the power station at Karvouno, the second the police station of the foothill township of Evrykhou. From there he planned to pass quickly to the execution of Greeks whom he would name as traitors, and he had prepared a written list of more than 200 who would be the first to be killed. As a preliminary step, he had got his courier networks into thorough order again, and was able to communicate freely with the new leaders he had set up in the districts, and they were able to communicate with each other. The central junction of the networks was once again in Nicosia.

He hastened the reconstruction of E.O.K.A. as much as he could, since he had decided to begin operations again in earnest if Nicos Sampson, the young journalist who had been condemned to death, were to be hanged in the summer. In fact, Sampson's sentence was commuted to imprisonment, and Grivas, with some relief, since his gangs were not yet ready, sent round an instruction countering the order to action. The groups were now to hold themselves in readiness, he said, to begin large-scale operations if the second Cyprus debate of the year in the United Nations Organization, due in December, was not to Greece's satisfaction.

In fact, the sabotage campaign started a little earlier, and once again succeeded in taking the authorities by sufficient surprise for damage worth £1,500,000 to be done in the first few blows. An R.A.F. Canberra bomber was destroyed on its airfield and four other aircraft were damaged, a broadcasting station was blown up, a merchant ship was holed as she lay in the harbour, and electricity transformers at the R.A.F. Station, Nicosia, were destroyed. Grivas's success at this time was the more surprising since the Intelligence organization had penetrated his re-formed E.O.K.A. more deeply than before. An important courier network was broken into in a private house in Nicosia, and documents taken that laid bare much of Grivas's plan. Then one of his own leaders changed sides. This man, Michael Ashiotis, was an area leader of E.O.K.A. and had been in frequent and recent contact with Grivas himself. When he gave himself up in October at Kakopetria, a mountain township not far from Grivas's own headquarters, he led security forces to a hide in which two other terrorists lay shot dead, and which contained pistols, rifles, a submachine gun and explosives. He also handed over the list of the first 200 Greeks who were to be executed in the next phase of the campaign as traitors. Two people on the list were found dead shortly afterwards.

Grivas was in fact preparing another round of sabotage, terrorism and murder as in 1955 and 1956, but at a more intense pace, especially after the Greek resolution failed to obtain the necessary majority at the United Nations debate in December.

Meanwhile, two things of significance had happened.

One was that Sir John Harding, the soldier, retired from the Governorship, having completed the two years he had undertaken to serve. He was succeeded by Sir Hugh Foot, the career administrator.

The other was that on 9 November, near the twenty-first milestone on the Morphou-Nicosia road, two E.O.K.A. gunmen jumped out of a small green van and fired at a car, killing the man who was driving, and wounding the woman sitting by his side. The driver who was shot was Mustafa Ahmed Beyaz, a Turkish police inspector, and the girl was his fiancée. They were on the eve of their wedding. The Turkish community of Cyprus, the leaders of which were gradually losing their influence for restraint, began to seethe.

CHAPTER XIV

B Y THE beginning of 1958 Grivas had lost his Cyprus battle, although he did not as yet realize it. After two military defeats in two successive years, he had reconstituted his organization of sabotage and terrorism until it was probably as strong numerically as it had ever been. But he no longer knew what to do with it. Throughout the early part of the year he plunged hesitantly from one course of action to another, never carrying anything through to a logical end. In the middle of the year the island was swept by a sudden flame of violence which, although it grew from the campaign he had conducted, he did not want or intend, and over which he had no control. Afterwards he flailed out into a series of quite senseless murders and ambushes which could lead to nothing but anger with E.O.K.A. itself and no longer had any possible political objective; they were the last irrational acts of spite of a tyrant who had finally begun to understand that he was not going to win.

It will be remembered that Grivas worked from the start to a clearly-defined plan. Knowing that he could not drive the British from Cyprus by force, he intended to fight a propaganda battle which would so influence public opinion, in Cyprus, in Greece, in Britain itself, and throughout the Western world, that its pressure would compel the British to surrender their colony into Enosis—union with Greece. That was what he and

Archbishop Makarios were after. Enosis, and only Enosis. It had been said a thousand times.

Grivas planned to achieve this effect on public opinion by three stages: first, sabotage; second, the murder of police and Greek civilians to impose a reign of terror that would hold the Cypriot public on the side of E.O.K.A.; third, murders of British troops and civilians, to provoke strong action in return, which would finally antagonize the Cypriot public and could be used to whip up a state of tension to shock world opinion and convince it that oppressors were holding down a slave population.

Always he was conducting a battle of propaganda, and the violence was simply a means to that end.

In Sir Hugh Foot, the new Governor, who took the oath early in December 1957, Grivas encountered an opponent who was willing, and highly competent, to meet him on the propaganda battlefield. Sir Hugh soon made it clear that he considered the violence not only criminal, but stupid. In private conversations, which he began to hold with Greek Cypriots of all classes in many parts of the island, it was evident that he regarded Grivas as an irrational, perhaps insane, certainly outmoded and, in a grim sort of way, comic figure. He dismissed the patriot-bandit-in-the-mountains conception as 'eighteenth-century stuff'. He, the new Governor, was a man of the twentieth century, in which one did not assassinate one's opponents, but sat down and negotiated rationally with them, talking sense. He moved about freely in parts of the island which were notorious for shootings in the back—in the narrow streets of the walled city of Nicosia, for example. He went into coffee-shops which had long been potential death-traps, and sat down to take coffee with whoever happened to be there. He took the risk, of course, of the odd madman—some crazed youth to whom Grivas had earlier given a gun—taking a pot-shot at him. But he knew very well that, at that stage, he had nothing to fear from gunmen under Grivas's orders. For Grivas himself, deep in his hideout, was carefully studying reports of the new Governor's actions and the happy reaction to them by the general public of Cyprus, who seemed to see at last a break in the clouds. He was quite intelligent enough to realize that to attempt to assassinate this Governor at this particular time would be directly opposed to his own aims.

What, then, was he to do?

He scarcely knew. As a sort of reflex action, almost irritably, he set his new-formed gangs to attack individual Cypriots with left-wing views; it was part of his make-up —when in doubt, to go for the left. They began on 21 January, when masked men slipped into coffee-shops in Lysi and Famagusta and shot dead several trade union leaders. These killings sparked off clashes between right- and left-wing Cypriots which continued for months, provoked several large-scale left-wing strikes and demonstrations, and a series of incidents which grew steadily uglier. The worst was when a well-known left-wing Cypriot named Savvas Menacas was tied to a tree in the churchyard of Lefkoniko and, in the presence of his wife, beaten to death by a crowd of youths.

The fact is that Grivas was so perplexed that he ordered actions of this kind which, instead of terrorizing the public into acquiescence with a renewed E.O.K.A. campaign, were rousing one section of it into physical opposition.

Things were not made easier for him when, in February,

Sir Hugh Foot flew to Athens, where Mr. Selwyn Lloyd, the British Foreign Secretary, had arrived for talks with Mr. Averoff, the Greek Foreign Minister. While he was there, Sir Hugh saw Archbishop Makarios. The substance of that talk was, of course, swiftly conveyed to Grivas in Cyprus. But for the general public this was one more hopeful sign that an end might be made. In such a moment, Grivas could start general violence only at the risk of having still more sections of the Cypriot public turn against him. He somewhat weakly called for a passive resistance campaign, and then, running truer to form, set his gangs to intensify the sabotage programme which had begun so successfully at the end of the previous year. It was mostly conducted against 'Government property'. This consisted chiefly of agricultural and road-making equipment which was being used in the service of the villages, as Sir Hugh pointed out. The E.O.K.A. raiders appeared day after day to blow up a pumping station or destroy a stone-crushing machine, to set fire to a timber store or a Government tractor or the records of a registry office, or to blow up an egg-hatching station on which the poultry farmers of the district relied. This campaign of sabotage, which did about £40,000 damage, continued until the middle of April. It stopped abruptly when Sir Hugh Foot sent a dramatic letter to Grivas, offering to come unarmed and without escort to meet him, and to give him complete freedom of movement for one day. The letter was sent through secret channels by Glafcos Clerides, a lawyer son of a distinguished Cypriot Queen's Counsel. The younger Clerides, while not himself a member of E.O.K.A., made no secret of his sympathy with its aims, and had defended many of the E.O.K.A. men who were

169

brought to trial. He tried twice to get the Governor's letter through to Grivas, and it was known at last that it reached him on 20 April. The sabotage stopped on that day.

Grivas did not reply to the Governor's letter. When he finally emerged at Athens he said publicly that he knew it was just a trap. To an associate he privately admitted that he thought the offer from the Governor was genuine, but he feared that, without Sir Hugh's knowledge, police and troops would follow to the meeting-place and make an attempt to seize him.

The real reason he did not reply was that there was no answer he could give which would be to his own advantage. Whether he refused or whether he accepted, he could not take from the Governor the initiative in making a dramatic move towards peace and reconciliation. He had lost a round in the battle of propaganda, and, deep in his hide, he was brooding on it.

Tension mounted in Cyprus as the question grew more and more significant. What would Grivas do? He had to do something, or risk losing his grip on his own organization. Attacks on left-wing Cypriots were not going to be enough.

A shudder went through the island when, on 14 April, a British police officer, William Dear, was shot and fatally wounded in Famagusta. He was the first Briton to have been killed for more than a year, and it seemed as though Grivas had made up his mind, and ordered another all-out attack on the British. But he had not. After the murder of William Dear, nothing more happened. Grivas was not sure, for one thing, that his forces were yet strong enough for an all-out assault, and he feared that another mountain operation by the security forces might strain even his luck too far. Moreover, he was still brooding on the best tactics with which to counter Sir Hugh Foot, who was now letting it be known that a new policy was being worked out for Cyprus, and, when it was announced in the near future, would give a new deal to the island. So the quietness, and the tension, remained.

It was to be broken once more shortly afterwards. Two British military policemen on duty in plain clothes at Famagusta, in the same area where William Dear had been killed, were shot dead by gunmen from a passing car. They were Lance-Corporals B. F. Turvey and W. N. Cameron, both young National Servicemen. When other members of the security forces reached the spot, it was deserted; only the bodies of the two young men lay in the road in the sunshine. Orders were therefore given for all Greek youths in the vicinity at the time to be rounded up for questioning, and 712 were brought in; those who were aggressive were roughly handled. A vast fabric of allegations of torture was afterwards built on this, but in fact only fifty-one youths had complained of ill treatment. Each of these had at once been attended by a doctor—some of the doctors were Cypriots—and the most searching enquiries revealed that there had been no beating-up, and nothing more than the sharp handling to be expected by anyone who tried to resist arrest from troops whose two comrades had just been murdered.

Once again it was expected that the murder of these two young soldiers was Grivas's signal for an all-out attack by E.O.K.A. But nothing further happened. The island sank back into the state of wondering tension in which it had been before. And the Governor flew off to London for final discussion of the new policy for Cyprus, the announcement of which was promised soon.

It was now mid-May.

Suddenly 1,300 troops in the south-western corner of the island raced up to the foothills around the tiny villages of Phasoula and Mathikoloni, about seven miles north of Limassol and not far from one of the biggest military camps in Cyprus. Tracker dogs went with them. Helicopters hovered overhead. Supplies to the most remote and inaccessible mountain areas were taken by donkey.

Grivas himself had broken cover. He had ordered several E.O.K.A. terrorists to leave their homes and make for the mountains. He himself, with two of his chief lieutenants, and escorted by a mountain gang as a bodyguard, was moving along the chain of hides that connected Limassol on the coast with the mountains around Kykko Monastery, which had always been his headquarters.

A wide cordon was made, the boundaries marked with tapes and lined with troops, the tapes being shortened every day as the cordon closed in. At night, ambushes were sent forward inside the cordoned area, and the two tricky periods were at dusk when they went in, and at dawn when they returned, and when there was danger of shooting at British troops. During the first nights there was additional confusion because a lot of sheep and goats were in the area, and in the darkness they were sometimes mistaken for men.

It took three weeks to draw the noose tight. By then it had closed on a cliff face that was so pitted with limestone caves that it was impossible to be sure of a thorough search. The cliff was therefore packed with explosive and blown completely down.

For a time it was thought that Grivas was inside and that he had been killed. In fact, he had slipped through the cordon by hiding among some of the sheep and goats which had caused confusion during the early nights of the operation.

CHAPTER XV

THROUGHOUT the E.O.K.A. campaign the Turkish Cypriot community, led by Dr. Kutchuk, had largely refrained from violence, but towards the end of 1957 there were signs that this restraint was not going to last. Leaflets began to appear in Nicosia announcing the formation of a Turkish resistance movement. News was confirmed that the Turks were also preparing for violence when four of them were killed when some explosive they were trying to mix in the kitchen of a private house blew up. The murder of Inspector Mustafa Ahmed Beyaz, followed later by that of another Turkish policeman, roused the Turks to their first serious displays of fury. It was Turks whom the police were now having to disperse with baton charges and tear-gas, but the leaders of the community were still, in the early months of 1958, able to pull their people back. The Turkish Government itself had by now taken up a firm attitude that the only solution to the Cyprus problem was partition of the island.

On Saturday, 7 June, a bomb was thrown at the Turkish information office in Nicosia. Nobody was hurt. But the bomb set off the most hideous two months of massacre, riot and arson that Cyprus had suffered since the start of terrorism.

It was not part of Grivas's plan. He did not want large-scale communal strife, nor did he order it. That bomb was not thrown by E.O.K.A., nor by any Greek. It was thrown by a Turk.

Grivas thinks that this was a deliberate act of connivance by the British to set the two communities at each other's throats, to divide and rule. But this was not so either. All available evidence points to the fact that the leaders of the Turkish underground movement—not the leaders of the community, who behaved throughout with exemplary restraint—intended to make quite sure that Cyprus would not go wholly to Greece. The new policy which the Governor had promised was soon to be announced. By acts of violence spread over three years, Grivas and E.O.K.A. had striven to make Enosis with Greece the only practical policy. The Turkish conspirators now strove, by acts of violence concentrated into a few weeks, to state as firm a case for partition. They knew that if the Turks, who were simmering with anger, could be aroused to all-out violence, the Greek population would reply with violence in return, without any stimulation from Grivas.

This is what happened. As the echoes died away of the bomb explosion at the office of the Turkish Press Councillor on that first June night, the Turks swarmed around the Kyrenia Gate of Nicosia, where their own quarter lies, stoning passing cars and the police. Soon arson started. Flames sprang up in a Greek cigarette factory. When the fire brigade arrived it was pelted with stones. The bells of the Greek churches pealed the alarm, and the Greeks came running out to face the Turkish positions. A Greek club and a woodyard went up in flames. Nine Greek shops were set on fire. Shooting started. British troops were, of course, hurried to the scene. They broke up the biggest fight, in which about

300 people were engaged near the Famagusta Gate. They manned the 'Mason-Dixon line'—the agreed boundary between the Turkish and Greek quarters of the walled town of Nicosia. Then came news that buses loaded with Greeks from outlying villages were converging on the town, so the troops also blocked all roads leading to Greater Nicosia, outside the walls. By the early hours of the morning the place was quiet, and before dawn the Governor could tour the walled city. When the count was made, two Greeks had been killed, many injured, and the damage to Greek property was extensive.

Next day communal riots spread to other parts of the island, notably in Limassol and Larnaca. In the latter town there were rumours that Greeks were massing to attack Turks, so some 300 Turks armed with clubs, knives and sticks marched on the Greek quarter; in the fight that followed, which was at last broken up by mobile police patrols, two Greeks were stabbed to death.

Within a few days the riots and firing of buildings were so severe, in spite of efforts to impose curfews, that 10,000 British troops were engaged in trying to keep the peace. Mobile operations rooms were set up, patrols were constantly out in armoured cars and in helicopters overhead. All the troops engaged were kept at high pressure for long hours, trying to head away from each other the mobs of Greeks or Turks who assembled without warning in this place or that, clambered into buses and set off to attack the nearest settlement of the other community. At times, conditions were near chaos, and it was in such circumstances that occurred the most horrible incident in this grim tale of communal strife. Thirty-five Greeks, who were discovered by a British police sergeant crouched in a position to attack a Turkish village with picks, iron bars and such weapons, were disarmed by British troops and put into buses to be taken to Nicosia central police station. It happened, however, that there was a Turkish riot taking place outside that police station, and an urgent message was radioed to the troops to keep the unarmed Greek prisoners away at all costs. By a confusion of messages, and a misunderstanding, they were put down just north of the Turkish village of Geunyeli, on the main road from Nicosia to Kyrenia, and, to cool them off, told to walk back to their own village, ten miles or so distant across country. Would-be rioters were often treated in this way. It was thought that the Greeks were by then clear of the trouble area and could easily make their way to a Greek village about three and a half miles away. In fact, they were ambushed by more than fifty Turks, who attacked them in the most brutal and blood-thirsty fashion with sticks, axes and knives, killing eight of them and wounding five severely; they would all have been massacred had not an armoured car of the Grena-dier Guards turned back a further mob of armed Turks pouring out from Geunyeli.

The Greeks of Cyprus believed, and many still do, that the British troops deliberately put the unarmed Greeks there to be butchered by the Turks. But an immediate enquiry ordered by Sir Hugh Foot established without question that the thing happened as result of a tragic misunderstanding between troops and police who were worked off their feet trying to keep the peace.

At the beginning of the outbreak of communal strife, Grivas kept E.O.K.A., as such, out of it. He watched it, indeed, with dismay. He was starting to see the dilemma he was in. His only possible course of action was to commit violence; that was the sole purpose of his organization. But once large-scale communal riots had begun, every act of violence, no matter by whom, made it less and less likely that the Turks would ever agree to Enosis of Cyprus with Greece, but would insist, to the point of warfare and perhaps beyond, that if there were to be a change of status of the island, the only one they would accept was partition.

As Sir Hugh Foot told Archbishop Makarios, 'Grivas is fighting on the wrong side.'

What he meant was that every act of violence that Grivas ordered would turn out to be, in effect, committed in the cause, not of Enosis, but of partition.

The massacre of Greeks by Turks was, however, more than Grivas could stand. Irrational though it was, he ordered in July that E.O.K.A. should launch into an intensive campaign of violence against Turkish Cypriots, and also into an all-out assault on the troops and police. He did not believe he was strong enough to bring about a general uprising by the Greek Cypriot population, but he might have come somewhere near it.

His orders, however, became known to the Government. Sir Hugh therefore decreed two forty-eight-hour periods of standstill on the island, with full curfews in all towns, no vehicles allowed on the roads without special permits, everyone without a curfew pass staying in his own home. At the same time there were widespread arrests of Greeks, and some Turks, who were suspected to be planning violence.

Early in August, after appeals from the Prime Ministers of Britain, Greece and Turkey, supported at Sir Hugh's request by Archbishop Makarios, the communal strife at last subsided. Fifty-three Turks had been killed by Greeks. Fifty-six Greeks had been killed by Turks.

Twice as many had been wounded on both sides, and the damage wrought ran into hundreds of thousands of pounds. Without the intervention of British troops, the police would have been overwhelmed, and Cyprus would have gone to ruin in massacre and arson.

It is a comment on the value of the island as a military base that, during the most intensive period of communal strife, it was successfully used for the airlift of troops to Amman, to calm the troubled situation in Jordan.

Grivas and E.O.K.A., it can now be observed, had been pushed very far from the centre of the stage. He made three dramatic attempts to regain it.

A patrol of Horse Guards, trying to carry out an arrest in the village of Avgorou, were attacked by a stone-throwing mob of villagers and had to open fire. A man and a woman were killed. On their coffins at the funeral lay laurel wreaths from Dighenis, with the message, 'Honour and glory to our heroes. I shall avenge your blood.'

This time Grivas was in a hurry. He sent immediate instructions to his killer group in Famagusta, and three days later Cornet Stephen Fox-Strangways and Trooper J. R. Proctor were shot dead.

The swift vendetta made such an impression among the villagers that Grivas decided to launch at once a series of harassing murders of British troops. He was prevented by the widespread arrests during the periods of stand-still on the island, for Grivas, his chief lieutenants and his principal couriers always ducked for deep cover whenever a large-scale security operation began. But he did contrive to circulate two threatening leaflets. One said E.O.K.A. would take a British life for every Greek

Cypriot killed in Cyprus, and this at a time when Greeks were being openly killed by Turks. The other threatened, 'bloodshed like never before', and abjured Sir Hugh Foot, 'Carry on, murderer. Your pillage is finished. Now after your debauch of destruction you must pay. I have given orders to all my groups to pay you in your own coin. My patience is exhausted.'

Whether he consciously intended the last sentence to be another classical allusion is rather doubtful.

He had, however, given orders to all his killer groups in the towns to start intensive assassination of British troops.

The first to respond was the Nicosia group. Sergeant Reginald Hammond of the Royal Army Ordnance Corps was out shopping in the suburb of Ayios Dhometios. While he was walking down the road hand in hand with his two-year-old son, E.O.K.A. assassins shot him in the back, leaving the terrified child crouched by the dead body of his father.

The following day Lieut.-Colonel F. L. Collier of the Royal Army Service Corps was watering the garden of his house at Limassol when an E.O.K.A. gunman shot him from behind across the garden fence.

There was one more murder, of a British police officer shot dead in Ledra Street in Nicosia, and a bold attempt on the life of General Kendrew. In spite of British security, E.O.K.A. men managed to place a mine in a culvert under the road just outside the British Secretariat, not far from the Operations Centre. They detonated it electrically just as General Kendrew's car was passing over it, but miscalculated the speed. The General's car was across when the mine went up; the following escort car caught it, one soldier being killed and two wounded.

The E.O.K.A. men who detonated this mine got clean away.

But that was the extent to which Grivas was able to carry out his threats. He no longer had under his command men of even the calibre of his first recruits three years earlier. He realized this and turned, as will be seen, either to softer targets or to fighting at longer range.

Meanwhile Grivas, E.O.K.A., and indeed Archbishop Makarios had been edged almost off the political stage. Nobody now spoke very much of Enosis. The question was rather, could a compromise solution be found that would avoid pushing the Eastern Mediterranean—and who knew how much more—into warfare?

Sir Hugh Foot had always maintained that there could be peace in Cyprus only if each of the two communities was allowed to manage its own affairs, and they came together to run jointly the common affairs of the island. Furthermore, it would be desirable for Britain to take into partnership, in ruling Cyprus, representatives of the Greek and Turkish Governments. This was, in essence, the new policy which Britain now offered. It was called the Macmillan Plan, and the Prime Minister himself flew to Athens and to Ankara to make it known to the Greek and Turkish Governments. The policy was offered for seven years, at the end of which they would all, in the light of experience, think again.

The Turks accepted. The Greeks refused (before the Greek Cypriots had even seen the plan). Sir Hugh shrugged and said that the plan would be implemented in so far as it was wanted. If, for instance, the Turks wanted to send a representative, and the Greeks did not, then the British would work with the one, and without the other.

Archbishop Makarios, in a desperate attempt to prevent the plan being put into operation, offered to give up the whole idea of Enosis, for which the bloody campaign of terrorism had been conducted, if in its place the island were given complete independence.

When Grivas, in the mountains, heard this, it was a bitter shock. At the start, he had promised to lay down his arms when the Archbishop told him to. But he had not envisaged that Makarios himself would consider giving up the whole basis of their desire—to bring to the Government of Greece that large population of Greeks who had lived for so many centuries under alien rule. He made to his intimates some disillusioned remarks about Archbishop Makarios.

However, the British did not care for Makarios's compromise either. They intended to implement their plan and to show by the steadfastness of their troops that they would not be pushed off it. This was it, take it or leave it. The Archbishop's suggestion of independence without Enosis was, no doubt, one of the courses that could be considered at the end of the seven years.

Archbishop Makarios then made an inflammatory speech urging Greek Cypriots to reject the Macmillan Plan. And Grivas, gathering his strength in the island, prepared to make his last violent throw.

CHAPTER XVI

IN THE autumn of 1958 Grivas thought there was one last chance of forcing the Cyprus issue by violence. Yet another debate was looming in the United Nations. The efforts of N.A.T.O. had been bent towards, and had nearly succeeded in, reaching some sort of agreement. It was therefore necessary to arouse the passions once again and give the final impression that there was no peaceful way out of the Cyprus impasse except by surrender to E.O.K.A. terms.

So he ordered what was to be the last round of assassination and terrorism. But by now the British were usually so alert, and the E.O.K.A. leaders upon whom he was forced to rely mostly so inexperienced, that he was no longer able to keep the personal control over the actions of his killers which he had previously exerted. His instructions were interpreted as a reckless order to go out and kill British civilians wherever and whenever possible. As for the attacks on troops, they were now chiefly confined to attempts with time-bombs, or ambushes with mines at such long range that the terrorists who carried them out stood scant personal risk of having to fight at all, let alone of injury or capture. The killing of Greeks by Greeks continued at its usual steady pace.

The assassination of civilians aroused, of course, the greatest horror. All who were to be killed in the last three months of 1958—which were to be the last phase of the whole campaign of terror—were unarmed. Several of them were elderly. Most were careless in that, being accustomed residents of Cyprus, they failed to vary their normal times and habits of movement—went to their offices, for example, at a regular hour and by the same route. One of them was a woman.

The assassination that aroused the greatest storm in the whole Cyprus story was the shooting of Mrs. Catherine Cutliffe, wife of Sergeant D. J. Cutliffe of the 29th Field Regiment, Royal Artillery. On 3 October she had been shopping in Hermes Street, Famagusta, with a friend, Mrs. Robinson, the wife of another sergeant. They were making purchases for Mrs. Cutliffe's daughter's wedding, and had just bought a dress in a dress-shop. As they came into the street they were shot in the back. Mrs. Cutliffe died instantly. Mrs. Robinson was wounded.

British troops then rounded up every Greek Cypriot male of likely age to be a killer who could be found in the area; and, for the first time in the Cyprus campaign, the Greeks discovered that British troops could be tried too far.

There had always been a danger of this happening, even though British soldiers are traditionally the coolest and best-tempered in the world in such circumstances. As Sir John Harding had said on an earlier occasion, when a bomb placed in a public fountain at Lefkoniko killed or wounded members of a football team of the Highland Light Infantry after a match, 'The people of Lefkoniko have reason to be thankful that it was British troops with whom they had to deal on that day.' Sir Hugh Foot and the military commanders had issued the most stringent orders on standards of behaviour under even the greatest provocation. There were, of course, many allegations of cruelty and torture. Some were of such a fantastic nature that their very absurdity answered them. But whenever any allegations were made, Sir Hugh insisted in having personal knowledge of the enquiry that followed, and the record of restraint was remarkable. There were a few occasions when it almost broke. For example, after the explosion of a pipe mortar at a lorry carrying the cricket team into the big camp behind Limassol, a number of troops, none of higher rank than lance-corporal, took enough explosive to raze Limassol to the ground, and began silently to march the four or five miles to the town. They were stopped by a sergeant-major, who, bicycling by, realized what was happening and persuaded them to return to camp.

In the follow-up operation after the murder of Mrs. Cutliffe, about 650 Greek Cypriots were arrested. All except two were released the same night. Two hundred and fifty of them were injured, and of these sixteen were detained in hospital, seven of them with serious injuries. Two Greek Cypriots died, and a British soldier was accidentally shot dead. An enquiry into what had occurred, other than a coroner's inquest, which could find insufficient evidence to prefer a charge against any individual, was refused. Grivas issued a leaflet disclaiming E.O.K.A. responsibility for the death of Mrs. Cutliffe, and the Greeks in Athens have tried ever since to persuade everybody (including themselves) that there was some other reason for the assassination. There is, however, little doubt that she was shot by E.O.K.A., in pursuit of Grivas's last-fling policy of indiscriminate assassination. Her killer was not found. And it is fair to add that Grivas himself had not contemplated the assassination of women.

But the slaughter of defenceless civilians went on, of the only kind that the killer groups would now undertake. They shot two old men of seventy; a prison warder who had been home on leave and was visiting a coffee-shop to give some Cypriot friends a bottle of whisky; three bankers or business-men who failed to vary the regular hours they entered and left their offices; a youngster who was walking on his regular route to work; and a church worker whose car was mined on the way to his mountain villa which he had said he would visit that week-end.

General K. T. Darling, who had succeeded General Kendrew, then put into operation some new tactics which completely stopped Grivas's attacks on civilians. To start with, he armed them. But that was not what did it. He worked out an elaborate system of house curfews for all Greek Cypriot youths which permitted them to get to and from their work, but otherwise kept them firmly shut up in their offices, shops or homes during the times that British civilians needed to circulate. To ensure that the youths remained mewed up, he took troop patrols out of the streets and put them on the roofs of buildings, in back gardens, hiding on balconies—anywhere where they could command, unseen, the egress of potential assassins. Since the troops were shooting to kill on sight of any curfew-breaker, the assassinations stopped. And Grivas had no answer to those measures.

The bomb was more difficult to counter than the pistol. Of all the bombing attacks at this time, the worst occurred in the N.A.A.F.I. in the R.A.F. Station at Nicosia, where on a Saturday night two airmen were killed and seven injured. The immediate reply to that was to dismiss all Greek Cypriots from employment at

R.A.F. and N.A.A.F.I. installations throughout the island, and to fly out from Britain R.A.F. replacements for the stations, and the girls who volunteered in their hundreds for the N.A.A.F.I.s.

But in the mountains and among the hills, and particularly in remote areas served by dirt roads in which a pressure-mine could be buried, E.O.K.A. was still able to ambush British troops—if ambush is the word to describe the traps that were laid at this time. The mines or the pipe mortars were put into position at night, and fired next day from a distance of about 700 yards, which gave the E.O.K.A. terrorists ample scope for getting away without fighting. General Darling began to counter these last Grivas tactics by flying, above road convoys of military vehicles, the slow Chipmunk and Pioneer aircraft with which the R.A.F. was now supplied, which could spot a running man and track him across country, bringing up troops to the spot at which he dived for cover.

When Grivas, at last emerging, claimed that E.O.K.A. could have gone on indefinitely, he knew that this was so in only a limited sense. So long as he was able to preserve his personal hiding-places, he could maintain a sporadic campaign of assassination, at any rate of Greeks. But his killers were being bottled up in the towns, and his guerrillas were steadily being driven to cover in the mountains. They were also being mopped up at a fair pace. It was in an operation around Kyrenia that the last but two of his original lieutenants, Kyriacos Matsis, was killed.

Matsis had at one time been the E.O.K.A. quartermaster for the distribution of arms, ammunition and explosives throughout the island. He was caught early in

1956, but escaped, and Grivas then made him commander of the whole Kyrenia district. British Intelligence, which had become highly efficient as the campaign neared its end, received enough information to mount a three-week cordon and search operation in the region of the Kyrenia Mountains—the smaller range lying along the north coast of the island. Hauls of arms began to come in, then more information, then the discovery of some of the multitude of hides stocked with weapons and food, and at last the capture and arrest of sizeable numbers of terrorists and E.O.K.A. helpers (including some Greek Cypriot policemen). On 19 November, Matsis himself and two of his lieutenants were cornered in a building in the village of Dhikomo, just south of the mountains. The troops knew they were in the building somewhere, but for a long time could not find them. Then a soldier, prodding with his bayonet, discovered in the tiled floor of one of the rooms a trap-door which matched the surrounding tiles. The trap-door could not be lifted from above when there was anybody in the hide below. But, of course, the men inside could not get out without exposing themselves to the waiting troops.

An interpreter was sent for and he called to Matsis to surrender. Matsis replied that he would send his two lieutenants up, but that he himself would come out shooting. The troops then withdrew from the room and the two younger terrorists emerged and surrendered. They said that Matsis had two guns with him and intended to make a dash for it. The troops therefore returned to the room and dropped a smoke bomb through the trap-door, which was still open. Then they threw in a hand grenade, which killed Matsis. The hide, when they came to examine it, was only 6 feet long and 4 feet 6 inches high—too low for anybody to stand up in, and only just spacious enough to take three seated or crouching men.

Such operations as these, of which the purpose was the capture of terrorists and, the ultimate hope, of Grivas himself, continued steadily in various parts of the island. But now suddenly, as Christmas approached, the whole problem of Cyprus began to change with startling speed. It was no longer on tactics within the island that attention was concentrated, but on determined efforts at last being made internationally to cut out this cancer from the body of the Western alliance. First came the debate in the United Nations, at which considerable sympathy was shown for the steps Britain was taking to establish a just settlement, and which ended with another rather innocuous resolution hoping that everybody would keep trying for a solution. But this time the resolution was generally heeded. By now it was apparent to the nations concerned that Britain did not intend a weak surrender to either side, but believed in the rightness of the new policy, and would implement it.

By 17 December the Greek and Turkish Foreign Ministers, Mr. Averoff and Mr. Zorlu, were having talks in Paris with Mr. Selwyn Lloyd, the British Foreign Secretary. And at that moment an odd drama was enacted.

There were in the central prison of Nicosia two E.O.K.A. assassins named Constantinides and Athanasslou, who were under sentence of death. The previous day their cases had come before the Executive Council and the Governor had ruled that the law must take its course. But suddenly it became apparent that the execution of these men at that time might prejudice or influence the talks in Paris upon which many lives could depend. After communication with London, therefore, Sir Hugh Foot ordered the postponement of the hangings.

Only just before the hour fixed—shortly after midnight—was it realized that there had been a misunderstanding, and that the men might be executed after all. In a dramatic dash by car to the prison, Sir Hugh was just in time to prevent the hangings taking place. Next day the men's sentences were commuted to imprisonment.

Suddenly now it seemed certain that there would be a solution for Cyprus. Private messages were sent to Grivas from Athens, telling him to stay his hand. When, on 20 December, two British airmen were killed and one wounded when a pressure-bomb exploded under a water truck, for the first time a Cypriot prelate, the Bishop of Kitium, made a public statement deploring these murders.

On Christmas Eve, Grivas put out a leaflet calling for cessation of E.O.K.A. activities on the understanding that troops and police would call a halt to anti-terrorist action. On Christmas Day the curfew on youths was lifted.

From the Foreign Ministers' talks in Paris and Zürich it became evident that the governments were now determined that the misery of Cyprus should end. It was upon the work done by Mr. Averoff and Mr. Zorlu that most depended; as Sir Hugh Foot remarked jokingly to Mr. Selwyn Lloyd, 'For Foreign Ministers, they were marvellous!' In February the Greeks and Turks, together with Archbishop Makarios and leading Cypriots, gathered for the London Conference, where agreement was to be reached; the Conference marred only by the disastrous crash of the Turkish Prime Minister's aircraft in Surrey, though, fortunately, Mr. Menderes himself was among the survivors.

At last Cyprus had an agreed future. As envisaged in the Macmillan Plan, the two communities were each to manage its own affairs, and come together jointly to run the island, which was to become a republic and could freely choose whether or not to remain in the British Commonwealth. Britain retained sovereignty over an enclave sufficiently large to support a military base. Both Enosis and partition were ruled out for ever.

There remained the question of Grivas.

Still hidden in some well-camouflaged hole, he still controlled his small band of assassins, together with a large organization of helpers and supporters, sufficiently supplied with arms, ammunition and explosives to continue guerrilla operations for some time to come. There was no guarantee—except his original promise to the Archbishop to lay down arms on his order to do so— that Grivas would come out of hiding, disband his terrorists, and accept the safe conduct out of the island which was to be offered.

There was some doubt, even among the Greeks, as to whether he would do so. At the suggestion of Glafcos Clerides, the lawyer who had earlier arranged for Sir Hugh Foot's letter to be delivered to Grivas, the Greek Foreign Minister, Mr. Averoff, wrote a private letter to him, setting out the arguments in favour of the agreement that had been reached in London. Clerides also wrote him a long letter of persuasion, and these two letters were sent to him by a secret courier chain which still existed.

Still there was no response from Grivas. He was

weighing up the possibility of going it alone with
E.O.K.A. Clerides says that it was only after considerable
hesitation that Grivas decided to accept the London
Agreement, and to carry out his promise to cease the
fight and to disarm when Archbishop Makarios instructed
him to.

At last he came to the conclusion that to try to continue the terrorism campaign without the support of the
official Greeks would be bound to end in betrayal and
failure. Like the Archbishop, therefore, he reluctantly
abandoned the concept of Enosis—the one thing for
which he had always been struggling—and tried to get
the best bargain he could from what remained.

He had by this time come secretly into Nicosia, where
he still had several hiding-places in houses. The one in
which he felt most secure was very close to both Government House and the Secretariat, and to the residence of
some of the British policemen. He learned the details
of the proposed safe conduct out of the island for himself and for any of his followers who wished to go with
him; and of the amnesty that was to apply to E.O.K.A.
convicts and prisoners. Much as he hated the basic
agreement for Cyprus, and bitterly disappointed as he
was to have been frustrated of his ambition to bring
the Greek Cypriots into the Kingdom of Greece, he
realized that the terms offered to himself and to E.O.K.A.
were generous, and that he was no longer in a position,
in any case, to refuse them.

He also assured himself that his fear of last-minute
treachery was unfounded. As he confided to one of the
Greek officers who were to escort him from Cyprus, this
was a major reason for him to remain hidden after the
London Agreement had been reached. He was at first

convinced that there was a subtle plot to trap him—
egotism, isolated with the wielding of power, can go thus
far. He was sure that, directly he showed himself, the
British would arrest him and find some subterfuge by
which they could bring him to trial, perhaps taking him
swiftly to England in order to do so. Or, if that had
become politically impossible, then he feared assassination; this fear has not left him.

Grivas was at last convinced, partly by the Bishop of
Kitium, that the safe conduct was genuine. He then
consented to accept it, and the amnesty for E.O.K.A.,
and to leave Cyprus. He tried to get permission for a
public and triumphal departure, for he was still doubtful
of his reception in Greece now that Enosis was a lost
cause; but this was coldly refused.

So, on Tuesday, 17 March 1959, not quite four years
after he had begun his terrorist campaign in Cyprus with
an actual act of violence, the Greek Government sent an
aircraft to collect George Grivas. Shortly before he left
for the Airport he appeared openly in his cardigan,
breeches, short boots, E.O.K.A. beret, pistol and binoculars—he had certainly not dressed like that during the
four years of his terrorist campaign—in a house just off
Severis Avenue, in the Nicosia suburb of Strovolos,
from which he had conducted his first sabotage operation
in April 1955. The house belongs to a noted Cypriot
athlete who was not known to have had any connexions
with E.O.K.A. In his house Grivas met and briefly
thanked the editors of the Greek Cypriot newspapers for
their support. Then he left for the Airport.

In the aircraft which Greece had sent to pick him up
was an escort of four officers, led by an old military
comrade, General Nicholas Paparodu, who is a literary

man and the translator into Greek of the books of Robert Graves. The officers had been specially picked because they were all former members of Grivas's X organization. Grivas embraced them warmly. He looked inhumanly thin, and his skin was a curious shade of yellow. Most people who saw him at the Airport thought he was desperately ill, but this was not so. He was merely very tired, undernourished because of the diet upon which he had placed himself, and emaciated from worry and anxiety, especially during the last hopeless year. All the way back in the aeroplane from Nicosia to Athens he talked incessantly. No doubt this was partly from relief at being no longer under cover. But partly it was because he has always talked a great deal, all his life. For a conspirator, he is very talkative.

CHAPTER XVII

G RIVAS received a hero's welcome in Greece, and was promoted to the rank of general (retired). His old companion of the X organization, Homer Papadopoulos, now a Lieutenant-Colonel on active service, was seconded by the Greek Army to be his aide-de-camp. A flat in the centre of Athens, which had been the Ethnarchy office while the Archbishop was in exile there, was put at Grivas's disposal as a headquarters. What it was a head-quarters of was never very clear. It was almost empty of furniture and, inexplicably, nobody seemed to think of bringing in a few more desks and chairs. Also, it was not on the telephone.

However, Grivas was seldom there. For a short time he returned to his little flat at Thyssion, where his wife Kiki welcomed him home, remarking how thin he had got. A dentist was hastily called to attend to the decayed roots which had perforce been left in his jaw. His brother-in-law, the doctor, gave him a medical examina-tion and pronounced him perfectly fit except for a lack of weight; he needed, he said, to put on about a stone. Old friends and comrades called in a perpetual stream; it is customary in Greece for even very senior people to receive visits gladly from anybody who happens to open the door. The place was surrounded by admiring throngs. And so, after a short while, Grivas and his wife moved to one villa and then another lent to them in outlying suburbs of Athens. Grivas was provided with cars, with a bodyguard of security police, and with several other ill-defined but tough-looking characters who stood watchfully around wherever he might be, and were cautioned never to say publicly where he had just come from, or where he was going next.

In between his public engagements he devoted himself to his stamp collection and to the preparation of his memoirs. He wrote them in Greek, for eventual translation, and in this task he had the assistance of several secretaries, among them Nicos Sampson, the young journalist from Nicosia who had been condemned to death for his part in E.O.K.A. activities and whose sentence had been commuted to imprisonment. Like all other E.O.K.A. convicts, he was freed under the amnesty. Sokratis Loizides, the original gun-runner, was back in Athens too, with far from pleasant memories of Wormwood Scrubs (though he thought Maidstone Gaol was not too bad). He was sharing the lawyer's office of his elder brother, Savvas, and seemed to have very little to do to occupy his time.

All the people in Athens who had been associated with Grivas appeared to be highly prosperous. One Greek newspaper, indeed, somewhat hesitantly published details of expensive houses and flats in Athens that had been purchased by various former members of the Ethnarchy, and expressed some interest as to where the money had come from. Nobody, however, was sufficiently indiscreet to pursue these enquiries.

Archbishop Makarios went back to Cyprus to assume political control from the Greek side, at any rate during the period of transition. Included among his transitional Ministers were Grivas's two chief surviving terrorists,

Polykarpos Georghiades, the inveterate escaper, and a lesser figure named Papadopoulos. Also in the Government was Andreas Azinas, the young man from Reading University who had played so important a part in launching E.O.K.A., and who had had to run for Athens, where he remained Grivas's chief representative, after his share in the gun-running exploit had made him a wanted man in Cyprus. Glafcos Clerides, the letter-deliverer, got the Ministry of Justice, and made an interested tour of inspection of the prisons.

The young men who, at the amnesty, came down from out of the mountains, the villages and the domestic hides of Cyprus, in a mood of exuberance and brand-new E.O.K.A. berets, had a high old time. A few of them had been in action with Grivas throughout. Some were E.O.K.A. members who had seen a little of the more recent action. And some were hastily jumping on the band-wagon. They handed in their arms and explosives (well, some of their arms and explosives, anyway). They disbanded. And then they got down to the drab business of earning a living. In March and April 1959 the unemployment figures in Cyprus, which had been an island of full employment, took a disquieting upward lurch.

The British troops who remained in Cyprus after a swift run-down in numbers tolerated with their usual good-tempered patience being spat at by street-corner boys and occasionally stoned by groups of villagers. They knew that this was only the hangover from Grivas, and that before long, once the enclave was established, they would be very welcome indeed in Cyprus for the money they could spend.

The more sober Cypriots were already starting to

reckon up the economic consequences of George Grivas. They had the first jolt on 27 December 1958, only two days after he had declared cessation of E.O.K.A. activity. On that day a Government spokesman, with the Civil Service's impeccable sense of timing, announced that the grave financial cost of the emergency had coincided with a serious fall in revenue. He said that greater financial help would be sought from Britain in 1959, but local people would have to bridge a lot of the gap themselves. So the duty on petrol and the cost of motor licences were increased, the grain subsidy was discontinued, so that the price of bread went up, and a stamp duty was introduced on land transactions. In the following few months the businessmen of Cyprus began to realize that the amount spent by British troops in the island would in future be severely diminished, there was some question as to who would stand the cost of the emergency, which was believed to run into several million pounds, and members of the Secretariat were now starting to bundle up the various pressing problems of Cyprus and hand them over to members of the transitional government. Moreover, the 1959 harvest, which began in May, turned out rather poor. Most discussions of this kind among Cypriot businessmen, once the emergency was over, ended with the expression of a hope that some rather vague sort of tourism would fill the financial gap. They seemed to hope that most of the tourists would come from England.

The spring of 1959 came to the island itself with all its accustomed loveliness. The snows vanished from the mountain-tops. The cherries blossomed and the bougain-villaea gorgeously bloomed. Anybody could walk down Ledra Street and buy the lovely hand-made lace of Cyprus without fearing anything worse than a sullen glance. In the villages, the normal life of work and relaxation was resumed. The ordinary people of Cyprus seemed to have come through four years of terror, violence, intimidation, passion and murder, with few visible scars. E.O.K.A. was disbanded. The anniversaries of the deaths of the assassin-heroes were celebrated chiefly in the newspapers. Grivas, in everyday life, might almost never have been. Cyprus was an island of peacefulness again.

Zacharias Karaphotias has not as yet figured in this narrative, for in the struggle he played a very minor part. He lived with his wife in the coastal village of Ayios Amvrosios, a few miles east of the little pleasure resort of Kyrenia. During the course of the terror, Karaphotias had passed to the Government information which had helped the security forces in their struggle to maintain law and order. He had then been kept well away from his native village, since the E.O.K.A. penalty for that sort of thing was shooting in the back.

In May 1959, when the emergency had been over for three months, Zacharias Karaphotias returned to his house in the village of Ayios Amvrosios. Within an hour he was seized by two young men of the village, soaked in petrol, and burned to death before his wife's eyes. There was a hasty disclaimer in the island's newspapers that this appalling crime had anything to do with the disbanded E.O.K.A.

The question is whether 'disbanded' was the right word. E.O.K.A. had ceased to exist, but its members had formed themselves into a political party, E.D.M.A. (United Democratic Renaissance Front), and on walls throughout the island both sets of initials were scrawled triumphantly side by side, just as photographs of Grivas and Makarios were pasted up together. Except on walls, this brotherly amity was imaginary. Grivas made no secret to his intimates that he regarded Makarios as the man who had betrayed Enosis—and, therefore, betrayed Grivas, who had intended by means of Enosis to win power in Greece. Makarios regarded Grivas as simply the tool with which he had prised off British rule. He had no intention of allowing him any further real say in island affairs.

Because Makarios is shrewd and subtle, and Grivas is not only inflexible, arrogant and an egomaniac, but the most inept politician in Greece—perhaps in Europe— Makarios was to be the easy victor, at any rate at first.

When Grivas first returned to Athens he was several times implored, publicly but unofficially, to lead Greece to greater glory. He replied so often that he had no intention of entering politics that everybody in Athens had little doubt that he meant to. There was some fear, indeed, that he commanded sufficient support in the upper ranks of the Army to be able to seize power.

Then the warmth of his hero's welcome began to cool. The single invitation to luncheon with King Paul was not repeated; in Athens it was said that the King was not particularly enthusiastic about General Grivas. The public began to accept him as the revered but powerless figure he had proclaimed he wished to be.

In July, therefore, he decided to improve his position in Greece by using the weapon that had served so well— trouble in Cyprus. He denounced the Zürich and London agreements, declaring that there were secret, verbal clauses of which he had not been told until he was out of the island.

To his astonishment, the weapon misfired. The Greek

Government sharply contradicted him, Mr. Averoff, the Foreign Minister, virtually calling him a liar, and referring later to his 'morbid arrogance'. In Cyprus, Makarios stood just as firmly by the London agreements, making it clear—though he did not name him—that he would tolerate no interference from General Grivas. All this was, no doubt, to be expected.

What startled Grivas was that his old E.O.K.A. comrades no longer supported him. Georghiades, his former lieutenant, flew quickly to Greece to consult him; but Georghiades did not resign from Makarios's Council of Ministers. E.D.M.A., the political party formed from E.O.K.A.,lavished compliments on Grivas, but came out strongly for Makarios, whose grip was probably strengthened by a sudden recurrence of violence in the island. Arms were being manufactured again in private houses. A bomb exploded in a roadside culvert in the mountains. A new underground organization, K.E.M. (Cyprus United Front), distributed threatening leaflets in quite the old manner—only this time the target was Makarios and the Greek politicians. There were allegations in September, indeed, of a plot, said to be inspired by Grivas, to overthrow the Makarios régime by violence. Grivas disclaimed knowledge of K.E.M. But the animosity between him and Makarios could no longer be hidden. Among the acts of violence, two Turks, one a policeman, were murdered by gunmen, and sections of the Cyprus police were re-armed.

Most Cypriots were so sick of the four years of violence, and the crime wave that still flowed in their wake, that they longed for Makarios to settle the country peacefully under the London agreements. But a small, bitter group still hankered after Grivas and Enosis. Their views were expressed in a sermon by the Bishop of Kyrenia, who hoped General Grivas would soon become Prime Minister of Greece, and bring the wind of real freedom to both Greece and Cyprus.

In Greece, Grivas suddenly burst out into insults, finding corruption everywhere, and proclaiming the country's need of new leadership. It is understood, of course, that his ambitions were, as always, for personal power in Greece, not in Cyprus; he stirred up strife in the island merely as a means to popularity in Greece itself. He was summoned to an audience with King Paul, who is reported to have advised him against 'inopportune' utterances. Grivas did not follow any such advice. Within a few days he was asking openly for power, throwing aside any pretence of standing above politics.

At this time of writing he had support from quite a large number of Greeks who were tired of the Karamanlis Government, and yet feared the left. It was possible that he still retained enough influence in the Army, and among officials, to attempt a coup. He has made it quite clear that, if he were ever to come to power in Greece— by whatever means—the unhappy business of Cyprus, where British bases are established, would start all over again.